Adventure Capital

Adventure Capital

✦

A Cautionary Tale of the Venture Capital Circus and the Clowns That Run It

Karl Capita

iUniverse, Inc.
New York Lincoln Shanghai

Adventure Capital
A Cautionary Tale of the Venture Capital Circus and the Clowns That Run It

iUniverse books may be ordered through booksellers or by contacting:

iUniverse
2021 Pine Lake Road, Suite 100
Lincoln, NE 68512
www.iuniverse.com
1-800-Authors (1-800-288-4677)

ISBN: 0-595-34461-5 (pbk)
ISBN: 0-595-67120-9 (cloth)

Printed in the United States of America

Cover Art

The cover concept and art were inspired by Ms. Latha Molakala.

Dedication

Although Karl Capita is not my real name, a lot of real people made this book happen.

I dedicate this story to all the employee 'sinners' who shared my venture Hell; to the friends who shared my pain on the nights and weekends I wasn't at the office but couldn't let it go; to my family, without whose love and support all I've accomplished would have been impossible; and most importantly, to my wife and to my mother, who both taught me that life is all about what you do for people, not what you do to them. Businesses might not have souls, but business people should.

Contents

PREFACE: *The Guilty, The Stupid And Me*

This tale is about one entrepreneur's experience with Venture Capitalists (VCs) and the world of technology startups in Silicon Valley. When I first began writing this story, I found myself bogged down in the long spans of business monotony that envelope the sporadically compelling events of pivotal importance, luminance, or insanity found in all entrepreneurial tales. It seemed more sensible to simply sever the extraneous limbs of a complete history and only present the key incidents as they occurred; this is what I chose to do, in diary-form: an attempt at reflection more than analysis. The dates and timelines themselves are vaguely relevant, but it's more about the moments, the snapshots of emotion and circumstance that really matter here. Each entry is contemporaneous; foreshadowing of future events is accidental, incidental or prophetic, though in each case no less telling on the outcome at the end of the day. I have tried to be true to my character and to those around me, but at times, events or people have been nudged slightly to protect the innocent, the guilty and all of us who lie somewhere in-between.

The story concentrates on the lessons I learned from raising venture funding; operating for several years in a difficult economic and fund-raising environment; through to our untimely but ultimate demise. There is no single reason or excuse for our downfall; as with any business many complex internal and external issues and events contribute to positive and negative outcomes. One element, however, was more contributory than any other: venture capital.

The primal force that flowed through our corporate lifespan, drove our strategy of operation, and eventually deserted us in dramatic fashion was venture capital. The venture capitalists we trawled for, the ones we caught, and the ones we should have tossed back into the sea, more than any other factor, contributed indirectly to our success, but far more directly to our failure. I employ those terms with reservation, as declaring "success" or "failure" could simply be defined to mean the length of our existence in an economy where many began the same race, but few lasted to see a finish line. That in itself is an interesting metaphor, because it sums up the venture capital imperative so well: growing your business for these investors is indeed a race with a finish line—the successful exit of the venture capitalist—as opposed to the building of a company that is established with no fixed timeline or end-goal in mind other than continued existence, revenues, profits and growth. For too many entrepreneurs (myself included), mistaking the VC goal of exit with our own of growing and maintaining a successful business was the most unfortunate mistake we could, and would, make.

This is not to say there is anything wrong with the venture capitalists' investment paradigm per se. Clearly any investment is made to achieve a return you can liquidate. However, when this goal conflicts with a company's own, and 'creative differences' arise, it is vital to recognize you are receiving partisan advice that is not necessarily in your best interests. When that advice comes on the heels of a history of corruption (financial and otherwise), you are in the situation we found ourselves in with our venture capitalists.

To be clear then, I am not attempting to damn the entire venture capital industry, but nor do I consider what happened in my specific experience to be isolated. The established venture industry before the mid-1990s (see discussion below for more on the history of venture capital) knew its boundaries well and thrived within them. Just as the general public leapt aboard a day-trading roller-coaster during the Dotcom boom only to recognize too late that they weren't the expert stock market analysts they believed themselves to be, many venture capitalists were simply in the right place at the right time initially. They were making money just like everyone else—on luck and an upward trend—only to discover tougher times meant they were in the wrong business. When true expertise and experience became essential, many were left simply scrambling to survive, unfortunately to the greater detriment of the portfolio companies they funded and who looked to their VCs in vain for expert advice and assistance.

I also state here—for the record—that I am in no way asserting that my own abilities, conduct or decision-making are unimpeachable. There are no innocent parties in this story. Whatever the realities of the market, the venture investors we associated ourselves with, or the condition of the economy and external influences such as the tragic events of September 11th, 2001, this was the state of affairs we found ourselves in and were unable to eventually recover from.

In my defense though, I offer the following assessment.

First, I believe my company was able to survive much longer and in far better condition than many others during a devastating recession and stock market collapse like no other in recent memory.

Second, despite the impoverished position we found ourselves in for much of our existence, we had our share of odds-defying successes, and were on the verge of a breakthrough that better support from our venture backers would likely have allowed us to reach.

Third, the initial premise on which we raised funds and laid out our business plan anticipated at least three years of R&D before a launch that would time with a then emerging market. We never had the opportunity to follow the path and the premise we were funded on; instead, we spent too much time forced to chase short-term directives from our investors with the expectation of continued support or new funding that never arrived.

That we were so close to returning our venture capitalists' faith and money, and were so unceremoniously hacked down continues to chafe, not due to some delusion on my part, but in the simple tracing of the history of our slow death spiral and how many collective moments there were to avoid it. I hope this book serves both as a series of faithful insights into my experience, and moreover as a cautionary tale to others following me into that big tent of the venture capital circus.

INTRODUCTION

For readers familiar with the venture capital industry, you can feel free to skip the rest of this introduction, which is intended to describe some of the recent history of venture capital and the financial markets, as well as the entrepreneurial challenges they gave birth to in the post-Dotcom funding environment.

A Venture Primer

The circumstances I found myself in during my startup career are likely to be familiar to you if are a venture-backed entrepreneur or a venture capitalist. If you're just starting out, you'll recognize them soon enough.

If you are not a VC or entrepreneur, this story might help explain why you're likely not as financially secure as you were in 1999. If you have any of your money in a bank, corporate stock, retirement fund, mutual fund or pretty much any other kind of investment, you probably watched in horror at the stock market collapse and "dot-com bubble" burst, wiping out what might have been an old-age nest-egg, college fund, or early-retirement plan. This story offers some insight into some of the practices and attitudes that made the Wall Street disaster not just possible, but practically unavoidable.

Most financial institutions, and indeed even public companies saw dramatic increases in value in investing in high-risk, startup companies (most often Internet or 'dot-com' related) and thus allocated some of their funds—your money—to buying into these companies. It seemed like a bright idea in the 1990s—getting a 10x (or even 100x) return on your money even though you invested in a company that had no clue how it would ever make a profit...or a product in some cases. Suddenly this did not seem quite so smart when you lost 99% of your investment and were not quite sure why or what to do about it subsequently.

In this introduction, I'd like to offer some thoughts on how this rise and fall were the inevitable consequences of the breakdown in the engine that drove the whole thing: the venture capital industry. And—worryingly—how most of the inherent problems remain due to a lack of any real oversight or regulation.

Pre-Dotcom Venture Capital

Before the big Dotcom explosion in the 1990s and associated growth in the venture capital industry, venture investment was a specialized, peripheral element of the financial industry, undertaken by firms that understood the risks involved, investing based on moderate returns (though higher than mainstream investments in bonds, stocks or commodities), with realistic timeframes between investment and exit. As a result, venture capital was a solid industry and a strong source of growth funding for entrepreneurs with good ideas and business plans. The exit strategy in these cases was primarily to spend a few years (typically three to five) building the business and its products, selling the latter and generating enough revenues to show a future trend attractive enough for the public markets or to be bought out by bigger industry players who could see the compelling value proposition. This applied not only in theory, but also in practice—something that was not to be the case in the next phase of the industry as the Internet boom occurred.

Dotcom Venture Capital

While the rapid growth in venture investing and drive towards IPOs and exit were not exclusive to the so-called Dotcom or World Wide Web destination site companies, this is still a suitable moniker for this phase of the VC industry as most technology companies going public during this period were feeding the Dotcoms in one way or another. By the peak of the Dotcom-driven boom, the VC industry had grown from $2.8Bn[1] in 1990 to over $106Bn in 2000[2]. No longer was the VC industry organized around understanding risk over a period of three to five years; instead, it was all about exponential valuation growth and churning out companies into the public markets and getting out before anyone realized what was going on. While this worked well for a while, the house-of-cards eventually had to collapse under its own weight and the added bloat of the ever increasing VCs moving in.

---

1.   I will use "Mn" to indicate the unit Million (1,000,000) and "Bn" to indicate the US unit Billion (one thousand million: 1,000,000,000).
2.   Figures from the National Venture Capital Association (www.nvca.org)

Post-Dotcom Venture Capital

The post-Dotcom venture industry can be compared to a recovering drug addict, in that it has two faces. The public face: the "what you tell your friends and family" side. An understanding that the last decade of binging was ultimately destructive and must not be repeated…your lesson has been learned.

And the other, darker side where you just know you can make back all you lost and more on one last shot when another buddy from business school is pitching one more off-the-wall scheme.

A technology company (as opposed to the website-centric Dotcoms) just starting up and raising its first round of venture funding in the latter two VC phases (Dotcom and Post-) primarily had two things going against it: first, its business would typically take around three years to flourish due to the technology's development-cycle (design-develop-market-sell). Second, paradoxically, an early-stage company would not need a particularly large sum of money to get up and running, nor would it want to take a large sum due to the 'dilution' or loss of percentage-ownership of the company that would be endured by the founders. This second problem was important, as the boom-years had led to local (Silicon Valley) firms often having too much money to deal with early-stage companies. This statement may appear strange and it bears explaining.

Venture funds are structured around partnerships, where each partner is responsible for bringing in and managing portfolio companies. The partnerships typically make joint decisions upon review of business materials and so-called "due diligence" or background reference-checks and review of the potential size and growth rate of the specific business and revenues. Venture funds function based on a management fee on the funds they invest, an annual percentage of which go to administration and operations (including paying partners' salaries). Where the real gains come in however is on exit of the investment. Venture firms buy equity or stock in a company for their funds. Their exit is through a successful stock sale, usually through the public markets after an offering, or through acquisition of the portfolio company by another that allows them a similar exit. The success of a large number of venture portfolio companies during the boom meant that venture funds were flush with cash to invest in the next generation of startups. While the amount of available money had thus increased dramatically, the number of venture partners in each fund had not, since the partners divided the income up, so greater income for a static number of partners made financial sense. As a result, six partners who had $150Mn to invest, with an average of five portfolio companies each filling their management time, meant a typical investment of $5Mn per company over its life. When those partners suddenly had $750Mn to invest, they were left looking at potential investments needing $25Mn. Early-stage startups struggled in vain to catch the attention of well-known Sand Hill Road venture funds.

Such startups were thus often forced to pursue two potential alternative routes: an "angel" investment round; or lower-tier, smaller venture funds that had cropped up as the venture industry expanded.

An angel round is made up of smaller, less formalized investors, mainly rich individuals who have made out either as investors or entrepreneurs in previous successful startups; typically these angels will take a bigger risk on an earlier stage company. These investors are generally a pain-in-the-ass to deal with, as they tend to be more "hands on". Translation: constantly hovering and worrying about their money and what you are doing with it, and often they want to inflict on you the pain and suffering they endured from their venture investors before they made it big themselves.

The lower-tier venture round is typically characterized by the fund being less experienced or often being outside of Silicon Valley and seeking to get a "piece of the action" that was enjoyed through the Valley technology boom and venture funds centered around it. The advantage of these funds is they will give you the time of day. The disadvantage is that they have about as hard a time getting a company to the "next level"—catching the interest and funds of the larger, tier-one venture funds when raising additional capital—as entrepreneurs do themselves.

Standard deal agreements exist between established venture funds and legal firms representing them and prospective portfolio companies, facilitating rapid closure of funding and getting many startups on the map in a fast-paced development environment where talent and even real estate can be highly bid-up assets. For out-of-Valley or virgin venture funds, such agreements and fast tracking are not established; valuable time can be lost on negotiating endless protections and clauses that made little sense and often are unenforceable. All these things are simply indicators of less experienced, less professional funds getting in over their heads. For a first time entrepreneur, it can be hard to recognize this, or to see the warning signs and understand their meaning.

As for the venture funds themselves, in a market where everyone had been making money regardless of what—if anything—they were selling, it was perhaps even tougher to realize that being a good venture capitalist is harder than it looks.

The first half of 2001 was important: it signaled the beginning of what was later officially characterized as a US recession[3]. The events of September 11th,

2001 further drove sentiment downwards. In such a time of uncertainty, investing in the future became an even riskier proposition.

It is important to recognize that a typical venture funding process involves multiple rounds of funding over time. Closing a first round of venture capital investment is the beginning of a long road that you hope ends in profitability. It is also critical to realize that profitability is not the goal of the VC: they are seeking a return on their investment that is not based on a share of your profits, but in the profit of your shares. The public market valuations of Dotcoms had much to do with the way Wall St. analysts and their investment banks were cashing-in while creating a buying frenzy based mainly on hype they had themselves generated. As the investment banks underwrote the public offerings of company after company, the analysts employed by them—supposedly neutral and balanced in their opinion—were largely pushing the underwriters' agendas. Much has been written about the excesses of this period, where a company like Buy.com had a public stock offering whose prospectus actually stated: "We sell a substantial portion of our products at very low prices. As a result, we have extremely low and sometimes *negative gross margins* on our product sales." [My italics.] In other words, "we sell stuff for less than it cost us to buy it." It's easy to see why selling dollars at a nickel apiece would be popular, but not exactly profitable. Should the public have read such statements before investing? Probably. But more pertinently, should analysts and underwriters really have been producing prospectuses in which such statements are buried?

In effect then, by 2000, companies that had been through their rounds of venture funding and were poised to IPO were the "Last of the Mohicans." The market was reaching the end of the glory days of "money for nothing," and as that IPO market (the exit on which VCs predominantly relied) dried up, the venture industry was about to come crashing down.

For early-stage companies just starting out, it was difficult to be optimistic in offering exit strategies for potential investors. The mantra of "we'll be going public in 6–12 months" had become as laughable as sticking ".com" on the end of your name and calling yourself a new-economy company. That this collapse came so fast and so hard was what caught everyone off-guard. Numerous analysts had repeatedly warned that the exponential growth in the markets was unsustainable (though many notably had not, as pessimism was not in vogue in the late 1990s). For the NASDAQ exchange, growth from a composite value of 740 in January

---

3. Official figures confirming the recession are available via Federal Reserve Board reports.

1995 to its all-time high of 5132 in March 2000 was nothing compared to the loss of over 72% of those gains 18 months later. The IPO market for NASDAQ offerings in 2000 (that last "good" year) totaled 397, collectively raising over $52Bn. In 2001, that number had dropped to 63, for less than $8Bn—an 84% drop.

NASDAQ IPOs in 2002 had dropped below 40, raising half of what they managed in 2000 when already in decline[4]. To put it mildly, the future wasn't too bright for start-ups planning to go public in the early 2000s.

In October 2004 the NASDAQ continued to hover around the 1900 mark, where it also stood in January 1999 on its way up, and in March 2001 on its way back down. In other words, if you bought in Jan-99 and didn't sell at the peak, you'd have just broken-even almost five years later. Suddenly even a 1% interest rate in your checking account doesn't look so bad!

Entrepreneurs were now forced to project a number of exit scenarios beyond the quick-IPO in order to still attract equity investment. The first claim was the "cycle," or the suggestion that just as the market had been high and was now low, historically the economy would cycle back within a few years and thus the IPO market would recover. Over four years from when startups began to seek funding in a downward-shifting, recessionary market, signs of a true recovery for IPOs are few and far between. I think even the most bullish of analysts does not expect the market to reach its highs of the past decade for a long time to come. Many remain optimistic that the IPO up-cycle is on its way—the trillion-dollar question of course is when will it actually begin?

Certainly the cycle argument was defensible when raising money, but banking on a distant economic turnaround that you had no control over was a tough sell to an investor on whom you were selling your specific business. Far better was pointing to acquisition by an industry leader who would pay dearly for your value proposition once established. Even this had become problematic, as a stock-buy-out (where a company would buy another with its stock as currency) was not what it used to be for both purchaser and purchased. Many a startup executive and investors beamed as their company was purchased for $1Bn or more in acquirer's stock, only to find that six months later, the realizable price tag was down to $100Mn or less as stock prices tumbled. At the same time, the acquiring companies had less stock-worth to play with. Firms that had made marginal purchases during the boom, erring on the side of snapping up a potentially valuable technology or service component in turf-wars over the virgin Dotcom landscape,

---

4.   All NASDAQ statistics and IPO figures from NASD.

now instead cautiously sat on the sidelines. With startups falling by the wayside everyday, it often made far more sense to let a company die and then pick up its assets for pennies on the dollar, than pay a premium to acquire an operational startup. The days of needing to hit the ground running to beat your competitor by a few weeks were long gone, especially in Silicon Valley, where so many of the collapsing companies had symbiotically relied on each other for sales, amplifying the effects of the overall economic malaise nationwide.

It was widely recognized that this shakeout had been inevitable, and would be beneficial long-term to the markets (particularly in the technology sector). Exit strategies involving acquisition by the strongest, largest industry players were thus attractive, as these would be the companies most likely to both survive and thrive in a shakeout environment. Pitching solutions that focused on meeting the needs of industry leaders had the added benefit that they flowed naturally from identifying customers. Any large customer became a potential licensee or acquirer of your product, service or company as they realized just how invaluable you were to their bottom line.

All of this was important when pitching to an investor, but these strategies were not simply for the benefit of convincing VCs to pull out their checkbooks. What was undoubtedly lost during the Dotcom boom was the concept of companies actually striving to make revenues and profits and wean themselves off of the venture teat or do more than drive unrealistic higher stock valuations in the public markets. Venture funding was primarily designed as a method to provide growth capital to companies to develop new products or services, increase revenues and build-up a core business. It had instead turned into a pyramid scheme with investment banks, underwriters, analysts and venture capitalists layered at the top collecting, and ordinary investors at the bottom, buying into a stock market with no basis in reality. Evidentiary in this was the concept of entrepreneurial "churn," where executive management of start-ups would jump from portfolio-company to portfolio-company, taking each one public, cashing out and moving on. There was never a goal to build a viable business, only to get to a lucrative exit and leave shareholders holding the bag when the curtain was finally pulled back to reveal no business wizard existed…or business plan for that matter.

The argument can of course be made that investors bought into this virtual boom and no one was forced to plough their money into the market, only to see it all disappear. While this is to an extent true, for many "stock consumers," their investments were made indirectly through retirement plans such as mutual funds or 401K plans via their employer. The loss of retirement funds have primarily been the most painful to regular, middle-class Americans, in step with these funds being the largest form of stock ownership for this group. What this market collapse has unfortunately taught us is that anyone can make money for you when reason and logic are thrown out the window in valuing corporations. While the pendulum may have swung too far the other way (bearish pessimism has certainly held back the markets in the early 21st century), the "new economy" has been thankfully replaced by the "new reality" which as many have said amounts simply to the following: "it turns out the new economy was just the old economy."

With the disappearance of "irrational exuberance" in the markets, to quote Federal Reserve Board Chairman Alan Greenspan[5], it is now more important than ever for an entrepreneur to seriously visualize a business plan that is not simply designed to hit the near-term milestones to close that next round of funding or push for an exit strategy as a goal in itself, but see current funds as a means to the greater end of building value in the corporation. That in turn should allow for funding or exit as a result. To paraphrase W.P. Kinsella: "if you build it, they will come."

Above and beyond all else, it is vital to understand something fundamental about the entrepreneurial relationship to the venture capitalist. This is something that for first time entrepreneurs is particularly hard to sustain. The company you are running is *your* company. Not in the sense that investors often use when you need their input on a tough decision, or when something has gone wrong and blame is being assigned (explicitly or implicitly). While venture investors may hold a majority of your stock or even control your Board of Directors, in the end, it is your dream you are pursuing. The converse however is also true. Investors love to push the boundaries of what an entrepreneur will do purely because they are trying to achieve their dream.

The investment atmosphere has changed a great deal over the past few years, forcing entrepreneurs to accommodate these new realities both in their fund-raising efforts and in their overall approach to doing business. The venture industry is by no means dead, but in many ways what has happened within it, mirrors the startup world itself. I think just about every entrepreneur has thought to himself or herself at one time or another: "I'd love to be a VC. Just sitting around listening to people's ideas all day with an arrogant, dismissive stare." What many do not realize is that the shakeout in the startup world is nothing compared to what is happening in the venture community. Venture firms are driven on the follow-

---

5.   Alan Greenspan, at the American Enterprise Institute for Public Policy Research, Washington, DC; December 5, 1996.

ing basis: they raise funds from within their limited partnership and from out-side—typically institutional—investors. In the same way as startups raise funds based on a track record of success in past ventures, VCs must show a history of successful returns on investment from their portfolio companies in order to encourage investors to place new money in their hands. Those investors in turn are seeking positive returns on the money provided to them, versus investing in more mainstream financial instruments. During the market boom of the late 1990s, it was relatively easy for venture firms to point to dramatic gains, and with huge returns to their investors, money flowed freely. Oftentimes, large institu-tions such as retirement funds move their money annually based on relative returns from the firms they invested in the previous year, always dropping the worst performers. When the IPO market collapsed, venture firms were no longer able to guarantee the kinds of returns they had previously achieved, nor were they confident in investing in as many new companies as the likelihood of successful exit had dropped dramatically. Venture firms could not hold onto this money interminably without investing it; nor could they take the risk of generating no multiplied return, or worse losing money overall. Larger venture firms began returning some of the funds placed in them on the basis that they could not reli-ably or responsibly meet the expectations of their outside investors. Smaller firms found it difficult to point to enough investment success to attract further funds at all.

The result of the venture industry shakeout has paralleled that of the startups it invested in. The strongest firms have survived and adapted, though not without the cost of reducing operations and headcount, and the smaller players—unable to secure additional funds from which they operate—have fallen by the wayside, or sought mergers with their larger brethren.

What is important to note is the opaque nature of venture investing and the decision-making process utilized by funds when funding portfolio companies. As venture funds are private partnerships, with limited outside investment from guarded institutional investors, they are not subject to the same oversight as com-panies in the public marketplace. The single, worst consequence of the recession-ary nature of the US economy in the early twenty-first century has been that it offered a convenient excuse for poor venture judgment. Venture funds that had made poor investments—funding companies with no products or valid business plans—were able to simply dismiss their failures as victims of a "bad economy." If using this as an excuse with their outside investors verges on an abuse of the facts, more dangerous is that many venture capitalists and their firms believe the eco-nomic downturn did indeed cause their portfolio companies to fail. As with any good pyramid scheme, "sucker's silence" works to the VC's advantage. Just as each VC in a firm does not want to admit to leading a poor investment, neither do the rest of the partners wish to be exposed for backing it. Protecting your fellow partners made sense, as they would do the same for you—no one could feel too confident about every investment they might have made.

Extending this line of thinking, the institutional investor who placed millions into a VC fund does not want to admit a failure of process or judgment either, in financing a venture capital firm whose investments are poorly chosen. Thus a code of silence extends from individual venture partners, to venture funds, to institutional investors and on to the institutions themselves that then drive the markets. As elaborate or conspiratorial as this protection scheme may sound, it was just good business sense—the market growth relied on an innate feeling of security and honesty from those steering the ship, projected towards the passengers: the general, stock buying public.

As long as the markets boomed and IPOs flowed inconsequentially, hiding these failures was easy—and arguably, if the goal was simply to make significant returns on an investment, during the boom these were no failures, since they made stock-gains in spite of a lack of fundamental business justification. However, just as one would not expect VC firms to invest in crack-cocaine distribution (regardless of how profitable it may be), a certain responsibility was expected—certainly by the stock-buying public who knew no better—in financing viable businesses and giving the public an opportunity to buy into the "next big thing." When the proverbial bubble did indeed burst, there was actually surprisingly little finger pointing or investigation given the loss of trillions of dollars to the citizenry. Assignment of blame largely fell on analysts who were both rating companies and associated with profiting from bringing those same companies public. And events were quickly overtaken by corporate scandals involving public companies like Enron, WorldCom and Arthur Anderson. More salacious rumors and investigations have surfaced too, such as the ones that indicted Martha Stewart. Her public fall from grace has been far more appetizing to the Media given her fame as opposed to an unknown venture capitalist or stock analyst. (Though Jack Grubman, the former Salomon Smith Barney telecom analyst with a $20Mn annual salary, may think otherwise given his own public dressing-down.) In addition, the events of September 11th and ongoing "War on Terrorism" have displaced corporate ethics and the economy in general as banner headline news, or sometimes as primary factors controlling stock market gains or losses.

Thus, between the overall economic malaise, the insider-silence and external influences that drew attention away from the matter (I will avoid even commenting on any governmental effects of an administration perceived by many to be more in-bed with the perpetrators than any in history), the now expired "new economy" largely avoided a thorough autopsy.

While this may sound like a fantastic conspiracy committed on the public by some mysterious cabal, with the exception of the loss of underwriting funds by institutions bringing Dotcoms public, most of them have done quite nicely despite the recession, with growing profits and revenues. The same can certainly not be said for ordinary Americans, like the near-retirees forced back to work when their nest-eggs disappeared with the market collapse, or the newly laid-off workers at publicly traded companies now cutting costs in lieu of revenue-growth, to maintain their "buy" or "hold" ratings from the very same financial analysts who were so wrong in their eternally bullish predictions just a few years ago.

Clearly, the market rollercoaster of the past few years has had dramatic effects not just on the economy but also on the people of the United States. And just as clearly, we can trace back the cause of the problem from financial analysts, to financial institutions and IPO-underwriters, to the venture capitalists. The analysts have been humbled, the institutions sued in class-action lawsuits, and the IPOs have all but dried up.

Only the venture capitalists have managed to avoid scrutiny, instead managing to wail as loudly as the rest of the populous that they are now victims, not perpetrators, of the past decade's boom-and-bust. We all must guard against them being the root cause of another one in the years to come.

PART ONE: Up

<u>March 1st: Pitching and Catching</u>

I know I should be worried…but it's hard to argue with two million dollars.

Still, there's something not quite right about this guy. When you go to lunch with a venture capitalist—a married, forty-something venture capitalist—and he spends the whole lunch flirting with the waitress and cat-calling female passers-by, it puts you off your food. It's not that I have problems with flirting as a way to deal with a midlife crisis. It's just there's a point where you start to cringe at the grotesqueness of it all—where you know even the victim of the catcalls feels embarrassed for the perpetrator. You realize something is not quite right with the picture…or the man.

So VCs are sleazy. I already knew that. But usually it's "just business" and I know they consider screwing you to be an eminently simple way of confirming they're getting a good business deal for themselves. Much simpler than—oh, I don't know—evaluating your business and the industry you are in and determining a fair deal for all concerned.

Oh but I was good today. No, not good—amazing! Yes, I do say so myself, thank you very much. Talking for eight straight hours after two hours sleep doesn't help the process usually, but today it freed me up to spout nonsense without being at all self-conscious about it. Two grande mochas—sugar and caffeine, the two wingmen of the high-flying pitchman—and I was ready to put that middle-seat redeye from San Francisco to Chicago behind me. And "me did talk good" this morning. Al didn't even have to speak. Hell, we didn't even need two of us to come out here at all—except as eye-candy of course. To get two million dollars, you need two co-founders to show up, as a wise venture capitalist once told me. With Jay back in the Valley, he might be good for another half million, sight unseen!

"Jump in if I get myself into trouble," I prepped Al, "or," I added, "if I look like I'm about to fall asleep." He was the consummate rodeo-clown: distracting the venture bull when I slipped or tripped, letting me pause for breath and allowing my brain to catch up to my mouth. For the most part, I was more than good though. "Sometimes I amaze myself" as Han Solo says in Star Wars—I threw out the line flippantly to the VC as we left today. (Note to self: quoting Star Wars is the best way of establishing your techno-geek credentials to a VC—thank you George Lucas and Harrison Ford!)

Al told me I looked like a cross-between a tele-evangelist channeling the Holy Spirit, and a guy selling juicers on late-night infomercials. Anticipating every question. Weaving glorious tales of future empire. Better yet, making it *their* empire not ours. High praise from a VP of Sales!

It started out with all the standard first-date stuff from the VCs in the morning: "What is it you do"? "Why is it better than what is out there already"? "Why you and not the guys down the street"? "How much money will it make"? "How much money will it make ME"?

The afternoon was different: the funding foreplay was getting hot and heavy. The last 24hrs were catching up: the lack of sleep; caffeine-withdrawal (even I had to quit at four Big-Gulp sized coffees); a heavy lunch, plus that vague nausea brought on watching a middle-aged man make passes at girls who could either be baby-sitting his kids or going to school with them. We were into the serious questioning: "How much do you need?" "What if we gave you twice as much?" "How fast can you put your team together from the day we get you the money?" Oh, and they wanted to know the technology. Not just know it, understand it. *Get* it. This is usually dangerous ground. Real technology is nuts-and-bolts and how excited can you get about nuts-and-bolts: as speaker or listener? Worse still, either the audience gets it, and that leads to more questions while they demonstrate how smart they are on this wonderful new topic; or they don't get it, and you're spending the whole time trying to not make them feel as stupid as they are—not a path to getting venture capital even if it is mostly dumb money.

Still, you can't argue with two million dollars! Well, a promise of two million dollars for now. Well, half a promise of two million dollars and another day of jumping through hoops tomorrow to make that half a whole. I don't need to like these guys personally, right? I suddenly feel like a prude. So the guy's drooling over women—and the odd school kid—walking by in tight business suits or short skirts. I'm not looking to marry him, just have him sit on my Board and attempt to control the fate of my company. Hmm, maybe marrying him would be less worrisome. Still, I've seen worse and moral bankruptcy is better than the financial kind, right? Personal foibles don't make him a bad VC after all; in fact he's been more than generous with his time and hopefully soon with his money.

"Money isn't everything"…unless you're an entrepreneur. An entrepreneur with a startup idea that needs funding, has half a dozen future employees waiting in the wings to join him—but not waiting forever—and who has been spending the last four months in a 10-by-10 room with no windows, two chairs and two co-founders. You can overlook lascivious VCs after months of playing musical chairs in a dimly lit box.

Still, I have a bad taste in my mouth and it's not from that hotel-bathroom coffeepot brew I'm swallowing here to keep my eyes open and finish this.

Two million dollars. We're a day away from pulling it off. I get to make my idea real. With real people and a real company. I always knew it would be a wild ride to make our dreams real. "Adventure Capital" is what I called the whole venture capital imperative.

Two mill-i-on dollars! Just keep repeating it to yourself like a cleansing mantra. And scrub hard in the shower—the dirty feeling will go away eventually. And then the adventure will begin!

March 2nd: Floating on Air!

It's almost 9pm. Or 7pm. Depending on whether you're on Central Time or Pacific. And I am floating on air, and not just because we're at thirty-five thousand feet. We did it! We actually pulled it off. I wish I had the energy to celebrate. There's definitely a party going on somewhere down a back alley inside my head right now, but I think my brain is already worried about how it's going to clean up the mess and scrub those stains off the carpet.

Still—absent my head jinxing things with its internal exuberance—we appear to have two and a half million reasons to be excited tonight.

One thing about long flights is they force you to replay your life—or at least the past day—in your head. Sometimes you want to, sometimes you don't, but it becomes unavoidable after four or five hours on a plane, especially when you spend the first one on the tarmac at O'Hare waiting in line to take-off. You've exhausted all the other time-killing possibilities by the time you're over the Rockies. Reading United's "award-winning *Hemispheres* magazine," from start to finish...twice—including the detailed explanation from the VP of In-Flight Catering as to why they switched from peanuts to pretzels and how this painful decision-making process took two years and cost seven million dollars. You've gotten over not paying the four dollars to buy headphones to listen to "Battlefield Earth" but still staring at the screen for two hours; and almost shedding a tear—that someone actually got millions of dollars to greenlight this movie. You have even wrapped up your favorite game of "fantasy passenger" where you make up an elaborate back-story for your life and profession that you feed to the guy next to you to see if he'll buy it. Depending on my mood, I either make up something so incredible that the poor java programmer next to me wants to kill himself for the choices he's made in life: "Java? Wow, I was going to take a course in that, but then this astronaut opportunity came up and now I'm a mission-specialist for NASA—I'm getting ready to go up in the shuttle to deploy a new spy satellite next month"; or so horrifying that the substitute teacher from Indiana retreats quickly back to her Fabio-adorned romance novel: "Yeah, I maintain the State's list of sex-offenders, but it's such a pain having to keep track of them when they move. They just slip me fifty bucks and I look the other way when they go to a new town. After all, they've served their debt to society, right?" Far more entertaining than feigning sleep or an inability to speak English for hours on end.

Sigh. We've started our initial descent after crossing the Sierras, but still over a half-hour to go. Okay, stop thinking about all the stuff we need to do with the money: find office space, get the employees on-board, get lawyers, buy computers, print business cards, set up a health plan and benefits…oh yeah, open a corporate bank account to stick two and a half million dollars into! Just revel in the moment. Just for a minute, savor what you just did.

Al is up there in first class (the biggest perk of being a longtime sales guy—premier membership on all the airline frequent flier programs and free upgrades on every flight) probably sipping champagne and having flight attendants feed him peeled grapes. Jay is back in the Bay Area probably wondering if we were just messing with him when we called him to say he needed to go buy a safe because the VC just handed us a briefcase with all the money inside. In neatly tied piles of unmarked bills. "Some sort of tax-issue the guy said," Al explained on the phone, while we both tried to keep from dropping the handset laughing. "I think he actually believed us!" said Al incredulously. And knowing Jay and his serious, organizational nature, he might be out there actually buying a lockbox…just to be on the safe side you might say.

April 1st: April Fools!

It's April Fools Day, and we feel appropriately fooled. It's day fifteen of "term-sheet watch". More than two weeks now since we got back from Chicago with the promise of two and a half million dollars, and awaiting a one-page summary of the terms. This was meant to be the easy part. The dragged out process is supposed to start when we get into the nitty-gritty legal clauses. But a one-page: "we plan on giving you the money" document should not take TWO WEEKS! I've heard "tomorrow" so many times now, I feel like Annie.

So we are indeed April Fools, and it being the first of the month, I have the fun time of explaining to half a dozen expectant employees that the check is in the mail again. There are only so many times you can offer that excuse; I just hope this is the last time I need to, not just the last time they'll accept it. One of the things we've promoted to VCs is that we can hit the ground running once the money is in the bank, since we have this core team that will immediately jump on board. We'll still have to hire additional staff, but we'll be far more than just three founders in a room the day we get funded.

The start of a new month—and being April, last year's tax forms are coming due—really reminds us all of how working with no income for the past four months is becoming untenable. Especially with job offers and steady incomes singing their siren songs to us alluringly. It's hard to tell a prospective employee to hang on for a few more weeks, days, hours, when the company founders are foundering themselves.

We have finally given the same deadline to the VCs that we gave ourselves months ago presciently without any VC on the hook, and reaffirmed internally just a week ago, believing we had reeled one into the boat already. No termsheet by tax-day and we call it quits.

The VCs took our ultimatum in their usual dismissively jovial way. "Relax guys, it's coming," they cooed. Maybe it's the engineer in all of us, but we are process-oriented. It simply involves someone sitting down for an hour and typing out a one-page document. "It's coming" somehow makes that process sound a great deal more complex than it needs to be.

So we are straddling parallel-universes right now. We are either sunk before we leave the dock, or we're running a multi-million dollar-budget corporation. It's hard to advance both scenarios at the same time, but that's the situation we find ourselves in. Let's hope not for too much longer. I'd rather be solidly poor than wishfully rich at this point.

In the negatively charged universe, we have the problem of having given notice at the 10-by-10 windowless-box we currently call home. We thought we'd be out by May 1st (which in retrospect was terribly optimistic), but on March 3rd it was a long way away.

Today we tried to renege on our exit and stick it out for another month at least—only the landlord has already leased out the place starting in May: to a French lingerie designer who wants a small sales office in California. For some reason the landlord isn't amenable to a space-sharing arrangement we suggested on hearing who the new tenant was. And adding to the confusion, if we really call it quits on April 15th we won't want the office on May 1st.

In the positively charged universe, we've been trying to engage realtors to find new office space to accommodate the dozen or so employees we expect to ramp up to in the next few months. We are out looking at glamorous buildings in exciting locations that edge closer to one founder's home or another, based on who is eyeing the listings on any given day. Since we only have one foot in this universe right now, we're using our early office hunting as more of a trial run. Looking at spaces that we really can't afford, or aren't likely to be conducive to our business. My favorites thus far have been the former motorcycle dealership and repair shop, and the two-car garage. "Great light," said the realtor about the dealership, with its floor-to-ceiling fifteen-foot high glass storefront. At least it had an office in the back—the rest would be an open range of cubicles corralled between a scary-looking bathroom on one side, and an even scarier kitchen-sink on the other. You could tell the sink was white porcelain originally, but only due to a chipped edge on which the grease would not adhere.

The garage was even better. "Well," said the realtor, "if you take out the garage doors and drop in walls with windows…and install carpeting…and build an air-conditioning unit and piping…and put some dividing walls in, it's a great space." "So, when will the landlord do that?" I asked, apparently naively, given the quizzical look I received. "Well, the landlord won't be doing that," said the realtor, "you will be." We wouldn't have laughed if it weren't for the earnestness with which the line was delivered.

There was a dreamy excitement about all of this, tinged with the fear that we'll wake up back in that claustrophobic office on April 16th with moving boxes to carry out the last of our meager office supplies.

The best way I can describe it is that you just discovered you won the lottery—but you can't remember where you put the winning ticket. You are mentally spending large sums of money and picturing your shiny new life, but there's that growing cloud of terror that you'll never find the ticket and have to research the most memorable way to kill yourself so you're remembered not as the multi-millionaire who lost his winning lottery ticket but as the guy who fell into the wood-chipper in a clown suit singing Broadway show tunes.

April 22nd: We are Legal!

We have legal representation! I can't believe I'm excited about that fact, but we're feeling good that with a termsheet in hand now we have qualified lawyers to tell us what's wrong with it.

Everyone told us we would need a good law firm, and we got one of the best. They are also the only ones that said yes, but we're not being cynical today. There will be time for that later I'm sure; they are probably already drafting an invoice billing us for the meeting we had today with the partner at the firm.

It's amazing how well the lawyers did out of the whole Internet boom. Certainly better than many of the employees and investors in IPOing online ball-retailers and sock-puppet pet suppliers did. It was a stroke of genius for them to start demanding stock in the companies they represented as a way of keeping their talent from jumping ship and working directly for their potential clients. Our new lawyers were some of the best at doing that: between IPOs and new technology patents the Silicon Valley boom had more winners than the 'techies' alone. When the tech bubble burst, Valley residents felt the elevator's stomach-churning plummet far more broadly than they enjoyed the ride to the penthouse. Lawyers, though, have so far managed to hop off on the middle floors of the house-of-cards as the elevator drops precipitously: working bankruptcies, corporate wind-downs and shareholder lawsuits.

Having had to face lawyers on the wrong end of a bogus corporate suit, I knew there are two types: expensive scum you hate [the opposing counsel], and expensive scum you love [your lawyers]. With our new legal representation, maybe there really is a third category: expensive non-scum. For a day spent with lawyers, I have to say I feel pretty good.

We did have to give up a chunk of our company today, for the privilege of paying hundreds of dollars a billable-hour for a service we only need because someone else is paying hundreds of billable-hour dollars to a lawyer on the other side. You have to admire the elegance of the scheme—getting paid no matter what. You draw up complicated, expensive contracts between two parties and collect your fees. Client wants to break the contract? Collect your fees. Client wants to enforce the contract? Collect your fees. And you know you're going to get paid, because who's going to defend your client if it's you that's suing them for payment?

Almost as spectacular is the business-school carousel that gave us the boom/bust spin of the Dotcoms. A third of the MBAs go to venture capital firms, a third to Wall Street, and the rest go off and start venture capital-backed companies. Funds flow from the VC buddy to the startup buddy, and then the Wall Street buddy takes the company to a ludicrous IPO, at which point they all cash in and the cycle begins again. But all great scams must come to an end, and now all those lawyers, who wished they had gone to business school instead in the 1990s, are getting their own back: suing the VCs, startup executives and Wall Street underwriters for all they're worth.

Success in business requires a great idea and a great network. If you have the former but not the latter, it's hard to get off the ground—this has been our great problem, as most VCs don't want to talk to you unless you're already part of their business-school club. If you have the latter but not the former—the problem with most of those IPOing Internet firms based on nonsensical business ideas but backed by the institutional pyramid scheme—you take off and soar on wings of expensive VC wax. And then crash and burn—or melt—in Icarusian catastrophe, because you never understood that flying too fast, too high and too hot can be fatal. But deadly only to those without golden parachutes that allow them to float gently and profitably to new pastures. For common shareholders, not only do you hit the ground at a fast clip, but you discover your wallet has been picked on the way down.

We've seen this all, and absorbed it all. But pitching a responsible company is not what this market wants right now. It's like an addict thinking about kicking their habit after a bad trip or an alcoholic saying "never again" after waking up face down on the pavement after a binge. "Never again" turns into "No more binges" and then into "Well, just one more for the road". For an IPO-addicted VC, that "one last big hit" is still out there and you'll just do that one and get out.

The longer you are surrounded by other addicts in denial the easier it is to believe those past bad trips were aberrations. This is the world of the venture capitalist today. The last place addicts assign blame is to themselves: until VCs take that first step of the twelve to recovery and acknowledge that they made poor judgements and irresponsible investments—it wasn't just the market, the recession, anything but them—we won't see IPOs and the venture industry truly recover in a sustainable way. There will be highs as they take new hits (let's hope we're one of them), but those highs will never feel—or be—as great.

The venture correction was probably more desperately needed than the market correction we've just had. It hurts to have felt the effects of going cold turkey on IPOs, but in the long run it's sound medical practice.

Right now I have a company in need of money and that makes all this theory dismissible in practice. Like all genuine entrepreneurs, we have wide-eyed dreams of doing things right, never compromising our principles and making the world a better place for our customers, shareholders and employees—and if we make good money personally, well there's nothing wrong with that, right? But good intentions and honor don't pay bills and employees the way hard cash does. A circus lion gets fed once it has jumped through the hoops and performed its tricks for the audience; so we'll play the lion, and suppress that instinctual urge to bite the hand—or the head—that feeds us.

May 3rd: Landlords and Other Evildoers

The local newspaper: the San Jose Mercury News had a great TV ad I saw today. It's purely visual. There are two shots that nail the Valley's current mood perfectly: they show a young techie-looking guy and then caption: "Yesterday you were a twenty year old millionaire." Fade out and then back in: "Today you're just twenty."

Everyone really did think they were going to be millionaire retirees before they hit their thirties. Some even thought they'd be billionaires. And a few lucky ones were, but not as many as are "just their age" now, as the newspaper ad hammers home. The feeling of loss is palpable. The stunned expressions of people shuffling to work and realizing not only are they doing so just for a shaky paycheck, but will likely be doing so for another forty plus years are everywhere. What a time to be starting a company.

Yet the hope hasn't quite died yet, at least amongst the professional services and startup-support industries that are out there still trying to make it big off of the backs of those still crazy enough to be starting something today. Everyone wants a piece of what you have, even if it's a piece of nothing right now. And logic isn't required when you're dreaming of being in on the ground floor of a startup that makes it big.

Take landlords for instance: they are living in a world where rental prices that used to be quoted in per-square-foot-per-year became quoted per-month, because the numbers just got unmanageably high. Parts of the Valley had higher rents and higher occupancy rates than London, New York City or Tokyo. And who was to blame for yet another exuberant excess of the late 1990s? The venture capitalists: they decided that blowing through millions of dollars extremely quickly was essential to drive a company towards a rapid IPO. Not building products or services, or even generating revenues, but being in an expensive office in a happening town, close to their venture brethren, and spending vast sums on looking and seeming successful.

Landlords were able to take advantage of the times, and with every company having millions at its disposal, why not ask for one or two years' rent as a security deposit, along with demands for company stock and excessive rents. When the collapse of the commercial real estate happens (and it will based on the way the economy seems to be tanking around here), I for one won't be shedding a tear when these same landlords can't fill office space even if they are giving it away.

What I enjoyed most was the reasoning behind demanding stock from a startup. The theory is that you are a higher-risk tenant since you have no history or stability. You could disappear at any time. So they need stock in your company as extra security collateral. The irony that your disappearance would make the stock completely worthless is not lost on the landlords; it somehow just sounds more plausible than simply saying they feel they deserve to be rich merely because you were sitting in a building they owned when you hit success. Still, it's hard to argue with that when so many executives and financiers who got truly rich via the Dotcom boom are no more deserving of their gains.

In our case, we are about done with our wishful thinking on getting a great office space inside Silicon Valley. We just can't justify paying five times the rent for a mediocre space compared to nicer accommodations east of the San Francisco Bay. But we are breaking the VC rules by not being near them, or spending money like we're already rich and successful. It's a calculated risk, and hopefully not one I live to regret. I do already lament the fact I'm going to have a long commute to work every day, but then again, I'm going to spend most of my time at the office with a lot of other people, so I'd rather it was bigger than my apartment.

We finally got around to visiting the bank to talk about opening a corporate account now that we look like we're making progress on the terms of our venture funding; thanks to our lawyers being experienced enough to tell us when we're being played and the VCs realizing they need to get their act together now that we have real professionals expecting to get paid soon.

The banking experience was quite revealing; I thought I'd give the bank my personal accounts are with first shot at our corporate business. The experience was cathartic to my long held sense that I was singled-out for poor treatment as a customer. They are an equal opportunity abuser, for business accounts too. My only rationale for using them is that they are one of the largest international banking organizations in the world—branches in every "citi" you might say—and this will come in handy in the future when we are the largest international technology organization in the world. Visions of empire indeed!

I began by informing them that we are a new business and wanted to know about accounts they might have for us. I was politely pointed to a couple of generic business-checking and credit card leaflets and the teller's (telling) look of dismissal.

"Thanks," I said, "but we're planning on depositing around two and a half million dollars into the account we open, so I thought you might assist us with that…but okay, we'll take your leaflets and compare them to the bank across the road."

A corporate banking expert magically appeared in a puff of smoke, and—shielding herself from sunlight so she wouldn't spontaneously combust or disintegrate into a vampiric cloud—proceeded to hustle us to her office to talk about how the bank could make our money work for us (though for some reason I kept mentally replacing "us" with "them" each time she said this).

I wasn't sure if the fixed grin on her face was genuine or not. Her expression was set like the consummate beauty pageant contestant, but something in her eyes and her voice suggested she was mentally feeding two and a half million dollar bills into a money-counting machine. Still, she played it cool enough to convince me that million dollar deposits were actually an everyday occurrence at her branch; and besides, they had this great promotion for a free hundred dollar gift certificate to Amazon.com if you opened a new account. How could I resist?

With an economy turning so sour, so quickly, I am continually surprised by the poor service that so many businesses are offering, when it would seem every customer is vital to survival. This is the problem for the consumer though—do you pick a company big enough to ride out any financial storm but knowing you're too insignificant to get their attention or service? Or do you support a smaller, hungrier competitor, who may end up starving to death and taking you with them? We chose the former, on the basis that even the smaller, hungrier bank truly aspires to be a large, dismissive organization one day.

In the end, the lesson with banking is as simple as it is obvious—banks are only interested in you for your money.

May 15th: Two Hundred Thousand Ways to Get Going

It's not two million dollars, but two hundred thousand is nothing to sneeze at. After explaining how we were about to lose our entire development team for the fortieth day in a row, the VCs finally decided that we were being serious. Two weeks of painstaking negotiations—that put the larger funding round on hold—and we agreed on them sending us a couple of months of money to get things started, as a bridge loan. Let's just hope that the bridge, which starts out from here, eventually connects up to a fully funded startup at the other end.

This is a very positive sign, our lawyers tell us, because this means it's only a matter of time before the rest of the money comes in. If it doesn't, then the VCs just had to write-off two hundred grand. Not the kind of thing you want to have to explain later to the people who gave you that money to invest for them.

My biggest concern is that two months of money mean it's going to take another two months to finish off the main funding round. The VCs assure me this isn't the case; we will be done in a month, but they want to be sure we don't have to do another loan if we go over that by a day or two. Sounds sensible, but then I've seen little evidence of sense and plenty of malicious intent on trying to screw the founders and the company in petty, trivial ways. A prime example being that we were all ready to receive the money on Friday. And yet here we are on Monday before the money finally comes in. On Friday we told all the employees-elect to come in today to sign their contracts and get on the books. And this morning—with no money in the bank—we spent a solid hour working out how best to cancel the meeting and tell everyone "maybe tomorrow" for the fortieth tomorrow in a row.

Armed with a wire-transfer confirmation, I finally felt some relief as I walked into our executive suite's boardroom to see a half dozen expectant employees' faces. I had just informed our erstwhile landlord that we would in fact really be leaving at the end of the month. Luckily (or unluckily?) for us, the French lingerie designer delayed her US debut until the Fall season, so we have been able to hold on to our box a month or two longer.

So here I am: running a real company, with real employees and with real money in the bank. Grins all around. I wonder how many of them figured we'd never pull it off. If they didn't, they had more faith than the founders had at times. The sunlight coming in the windows couldn't compare to the light I was exuding simply knowing we were renting this boardroom for the last time, and I didn't have to worry about how we'd be paying for it either.

Beyond signing everyone up as an employee, we had a lot to do, and we needed engineers, marketing specialists and management to pitch in on grunt work, regardless of whether we were engineering, marketing or managing it. The enthusiasm with which everyone jumped to volunteer as I read out my task-list made me feel like this was going to work. We're a real team. More than that, we're a family. The bond is strong: constructed out of all these people waiting unwearyingly and optimistically, combined with the founders delivering on our promise that their patience would be rewarded.

Going through our budget, two hundred thousand dollars doesn't go as far as you'd think. Between salaries for the employees (the VCs gallantly volunteered that the founders would not be paid until we closed the final funding), and buying equipment and setting up benefits, the money looks like it'll be depleting rapidly. But we are fiscally responsible business-owners now, and we will last a full two months, just as the plan calls for. (Though we could only last a couple of days after that without more money; still, expectations are high that we're just a few weeks away from closing now.)

Priority-one is to find new digs. When we called the realtor today to tell him we had money in the bank, he suddenly had a bunch of new listings to show us. I guess he knows we're not just tire-kicking anymore, so we're getting to see the good stuff now. There already look like a couple of fine prospects—thirty miles from home, but a third of the cost of the space I initially had my heart set on which was a block from my apartment.

A friend of mine called today to congratulate me, and cooed over how cool it must be to be your own boss. And it is—but only for the brief moments that you have an opportunity to stop and think about it. The rest of the time you are trying to solve four simultaneous problems while calculating in which order you need to call the six people waiting to hear from you, and work out which friends or family will be least upset when you blow off the plans you made with them. But you know what? It is cool, because you're doing all this for the person you care about most—yourself. (I don't have a wife and kids, so I don't need to nobly pretend I'm doing it for them.)

I've made a promise to myself that no matter what happens—even if we degenerate into catastrophic failure two months, two years or decades from now—I will always take pleasure in the overall experience, even if I end up stressed-out or miserable about something specific.

Misery begins for real tomorrow, when I get back on the funding horse. We have two hundred thousand dollars today, but beyond getting us up-and-running, my main job now is to get the other two point three million into the hands of our now two-hundred thousand times friendlier bank manager.

May 29th: Making Payroll

I signed my first paychecks today. We did them by hand as we're still finalizing a payroll and benefits system. It didn't really strike me until today that I am (temporarily at least) responsible for the livelihood of every one of these people whose check I just put my signature on.

It's a humbling responsibility. As an employee, you rarely think about everything it takes to make sure you get your check every two weeks—it just shows up in your bank account. But as I'm sure small business owners already know and I'm just discovering, there's something about potentially screwing up someone else's life-plan-dream if you can't pay them on time that is very different from accepting that risk yourself.

At some point a company clearly gets too big to think of employees as individuals with lives, plans, dreams. You couldn't cut thousands of jobs or shutdown plants and shift the jobs overseas if you thought about what it did to the individuals you laid off. I tell myself I'll never be that way, but know that every business owner or CEO must say that; at some point circumstances or the individual change enough for it to happen with regularity. So perhaps the same will happen to me one day (I can only dream about heading an organization so big as to be laying off dozens never mind thousands). But I promise to remember the sense of accomplishment and responsibility I have today and how much they mean to me and to the employees, as I pass out those first half-dozen hand-drafted checks to my startup family.

June 3rd: One Smart VC

I can't decide if venture capitalists are stupid, evil, or both. Our lead VC is most certainly both. Beyond the personal sleaziness, he takes every opportunity to dissemble, cheat, scam or delay us. For this, he is most certainly evil. The fact that he is now a part owner of the company through his bridge loan—whose interest gets repaid in corporate stock—makes it all the stranger that he'd attempt to derail us. This makes him stupid.

We have a secondary investor, who took us from two million dollars in funding to two-and-a-half; he is most definitely not stupid and I can't really call him evil either. This has been quite a revelation, because I have—without fail—been able to place every other VC I've met into one of those two categories. I cheat a bit by saying anyone who didn't "get it" when we pitched to them and turned us down for an investment must be stupid. For the most part though, it's the reasons for rejecting us (or lack thereof), or the lines of VC questioning during the process that establish their stupidity in my mind.

I remember putting up a chart of historical growth in our industry that had the present number of users in the world at just under a billion. The VC said: "But when's it going to become a viable market?"

I paused for several seconds formulating an answer that didn't involve screaming and running around the room like Daffy Duck on steroids: "Well, the market has doubled in the last two years, so now one in every six people on the planet owns one of these things we'll be selling stuff for."

"So, when do you think it'll reach viability based on that growth?" The VC looked pleased with herself that she was able to ask what seemed to be an intelligent, relevant question.

I pictured a dog-eared copy of "Venture Capital for Dummies" in her desk drawer, with the "questions that make you seem smart" page bookmarked.

"Oh, I'm guessing about TWO YEARS AGO!" I wanted to bellow. Instead, I simply threw out an answer she wanted to hear, she mentally checked off that her question was answered, and I went through the motions of finishing a pitch I knew had no chance of success, or if it did, having an investor too stupid to bring any value…except for her checkbook.

As a non-American, the media here has always fascinated me: how they strive to reduce everything to sound bites and headlines. There's no depth to the stories—no getting to the hard facts. Just something that sounds good and is memorable beyond the usual minute attention span that the media themselves seem to have bred into the populous. Venture capital has taken this Attention Deficit

Disorder to epidemic levels. It begins with demands for "elevator pitches" (sell your business in less than thirty seconds, as if you're riding up in an elevator with a VC and this is your only chance to get him to invest). Not in itself a bad idea: can you describe what you do concisely? But the formula stresses style over substance to the point that it doesn't matter what the words are or what they mean, only how slickly they are strung together, and how alluringly they are delivered.

For an elevator pitch to be successful, you need your audience to be captivated by your opening line. A lot like trying to pick up at a bar, only more sordid because the person you're trying to pick up already knows you're going to put out on the first date—they don't need to bother with dinner or drinks.

Why is that established network of business-school buddies so important? Your audience is captivated before you walk into the bar, so you just need to stick your underwear and room-key on the table and the VC will be up in a minute.

The other allusion to the American media is in meetings with VCs. Journalists ask a question (sometimes intelligent, but often not), get a non-responsive answer, and then simply move onto the next question. At the end of the interview, they look at their notes, confirm they've asked every question on the list, and conclude they've done their job.

So venture capitalists would make good journalists (or bad journalists technically, but clearly employable journalists in any case); and they'd make great advertising execs, with their apparent capability to determine a great thirty-second ad, brand or slogan; but do they make good financial investors? My experience and my gut say in large part that they do not. The real research and analysis on a business is done by the unsung Venture Associates, who do all the legwork behind the scenes to understand an industry and what might work and what will fail within. But they don't make decisions and the best representations from the associate are far outweighed by the buddy system and the personal connection a VC feels for the entrepreneur.

The problem with this thesis for most venture capitalists—and I'm sure any reading this diary would immediately point this out—is that they have made a lot of money, and success is the leading indicator of capability and intelligence.

A market that made no sense and ended up as nonsense, the Dotcom boom, and "irrational exuberance" (as Alan Greenspan once said) all made capability and intelligence worthless. In fact, many an institutional fund manager found themselves out of a job because they failed to jump on the Internet bandwagon and bring in vast returns, simply because they looked at the fundamentals and said this was all fantasy. It took time for someone to point out that the Emperor was naked, but everyone was merrily praising the finery of his clothes for a while first.

The true indicator of a good venture capitalist is in how they fare with negative market conditions and what appears to be an "irrational depression" that we are seeing now. For the most part, VCs are crawling into hibernation, tossing back masses of money to their own investors, not knowing how to pick a winner when the race isn't rigged so everyone's a winner anymore.

So here we are trying to raise money in this climate. I'm being too uncharitable to our lead investor since he's actually willing to invest, and can recognize a good company when he sees one, since he's putting his money into us. And he was atypical because he went beyond an elevator-pitch and gave us time to explain our idea, and was not afraid of letting us know he was getting an education on our industry. While some of his personal traits set off alarm bells, he was not a stupid evaluator. Again, his stupidity has been subsequent, when he has made the decision to invest, but cannot seem to part with the money, knowing that every day he delays we grow weaker simply by treading water.

As for our secondary investor: he's fond of lamenting to us that there's little he can do to push the lead investor to a conclusion. You can nudge and cajole, but he's the one who's dishing out most of the money, so you can't take him out of his comfort zone. It's impolite to complain about not being in first class, when the other guy is paying for your ticket.

Still, I feel a lot better knowing we have one of the good guys as an investor, and soon to be sitting on our board. Not that he's a pushover, but he truly believes what is good for the company is good for him and he understands what's good for the company.

I was wrong: not every VC is stupid, evil or both.

June 12th: Pond Scum

It's been yet another day spending ten hours pouring over pages of legal clauses; and then fitting in another ten hours of getting the company up and running.

At least we've found a home. Finally. It's a great building, with two floors of individual offices; a basement that we can banish the employees we hate to; and a wraparound balcony that on a non-'spare-the-air' day, you can just about see the San Francisco Bay.

It came close to never happening though. We had chosen a charmless, modern space, in a charmless modern building and resigned ourselves to the fact that this is all we could really afford. "You've got to see this place," said the delegated employee who had been out to see our future offices: "it's beautiful." At some point though, you have to make a decision, and I had drawn the line yesterday. But she begged me to go check it out, and I fell in love with the place immediately. Not exactly where you'd picture a high tech company, it was wood and tile and in an historic district. But it's cheap by the square-foot, and it really is beautiful. It also gives us great space to expand into as we grow.

For now though, it's more expensive, and we're going to have to try to sublease, and that's a headache I could do without. Maybe we can turn into a venture incubator, hosting lots of other little startups, and demanding outrageous stock and rent from them, just as our landlords-in-waiting attempted to extract from us. But they know they're in a bind, because the place has been dormant for a while now. The negotiation went a bit like this:

"We will rent the place to you, but you need to give us stock in the company, and one year's rent as a security deposit."

"Okay, well, we can give you two months of rent as a security deposit, and no stock."

"But we MUST have stock and a bigger deposit, because it's a risk for us renting to a startup company with no history."

"Okay, well, we will give you two months of rent as a security deposit and no stock."

"Agreed. When can you move in?"

Having a home is a big weight off my mind, while I decipher the cryptic demands of our investors and close our funding round. As we spin our wheels relentlessly day after day on ridiculous legalese, it allows me to retain a sense that we are still making progress as a real company, if not as a funded one that will last beyond the next month.

We're about to process our second payroll, and in this past month of me working on closing funding everyday, we still don't have a first full draft of documents. And there is only one reason for that, and it is our investors' lawyer, who I will simultaneously protect and describe perfectly by using the pseudonym "Dick".

Dick is a lawyer, so he's starting from a suspect gene pool, but in the echelons of scum, he can only dream of being from a pond. When other lawyers are saying you're bad, there must be a serious problem; he has managed to drive me to the brink of insanity for almost two months. I feel compelled to document his three best moments here and now, and then I will simply hope we are done in the next week or so, and are rid of him forever.

Dick is a partner in the office of a Chicago Illinois law firm. Perhaps they do things differently there than in California. By "there" I mean in Dick's office, because they don't in Illinois, in Chicago or at his law firm. Partners in law firms are expensive commodities; our firm—trying to be practical and save us some money—assigned a senior associate to work on our funding close. After all, you don't need a partner to do the legwork: unless you are Dick. So yes, our VCs' lawyer was overcharging us—and by extension them, since it's all their money at the end of the day; but this was not what had me alternately laughing and crying. Dick—as a partner—refused to speak to our senior associate. She called to let me know why we were delayed: "Apparently, partners can only talk to partners, not to associates," she explained. "Is that true?" I asked. "Not in any law firm in the country that I've ever worked with, no," she admitted: "but Dick says there's a protocol." "Is there a protocol?" I asked already knowing the answer. "Not in any law firm in the country that I've ever dealt with, no," she said: "but Dick says he went to Yale Law School and that's how they do things." "Do they do things like that at Yale Law School?" I asked, again knowing the answer. "Well, I asked around to some of the Yale grads we have here at the office, and they all had a good laugh about it—they were waiting for the punch line of the joke." I sighed: "And let me guess, the punch line was: 'I'm not joking', right?" It took about three days to straighten out an arrangement whereby our partner organized a phone-meeting between partners, to introduce his senior associate, and then hand-off day-to-day operations to her, while assuring Dick that he would be included on all correspondence and was personally approving all communications back-and-forth. "What a Dick" was all he'd say to me about the whole thing later.

As we're into the twenty-first century, the legal profession like almost all others has embraced technological advances like the word processor. Given the law is all about documenting agreements, Microsoft Word has become a valued and essential tool to business. Except for Dick. He has decided that the way to edit documents is by having our lawyers fax him the pages, so he can scrawl handwritten notes in the margins, and then fax them back, just to be sure they are unintelligible. I'm not quite sure how traumatic the switch was from carrier pigeon to employing the facsimile machine, but he appears to be taking it out on us.

The legal associate who is managing our funding-close seemed aggrieved at the stupidity of this editing methodology; she is used to sending and receiving Word documents with the "Track Changes" option turned on, so it takes seconds to agree or disagree to modifications, and produce a redline-document you can peruse rapidly. She made the mistake of asking Dick to end the use of fax-scrawl. Dick accommodated her—by resorting to simply dictating his language changes over the phone. Not explicitly, but in vague ways whereby he would say: "I don't like this clause. Change it to protect my client better." The associate would attempt to psychically-channel his intent and send out another draft. "No, that's not what I meant. Try again," would come the response. In the meantime, we'd have lost another day in the process.

Eventually, the associate registered a complaint to the partner, who passed it on to me, and I then made the stupid mistake of shooting Dick an email. A bad mistake: Dick informed me in no uncertain terms that it was "an outrage" that I would be contacting "opposing counsel" directly. Attempts to explain that I'm simply trying to drive the process forward, not actually discussing any legal matters were rebuffed. After apologizing profusely, it struck me that I had no idea why I should be sorry. Calls were made to the VCs and my rage grew as I recounted each incident that brought us to this point. Maybe it was the threat of walking away, more likely it was my repeated reminder that two hundred thousand dollars was going to be the cost of this two-month disaster to our investors while I would happily just walk away and get a job; in any case, I was called shortly thereafter by an amused legal associate who had received an edited Word document with the first modification being the word: "Sorry".

Today, we had the undisputed Number One from Dick's Greatest Hits album, and this is what's made me finally replay all those other memorable tracks. We've actually gotten pretty close to being done, with all the major negotiations complete and fundamentals agreed to. There are perhaps a half-dozen clauses still to be decided, most of which are related to California law that Dick and our VCs—being from outside CA—are not aware of. A good example is that CA does not uphold non-compete clauses, since so many specialized technology employees have a limited number of companies they can actually work for, and a non-compete would effectively stop them from being employed at all. Our lawyers have explained that a non-compete clause is thus unenforceable, and in fact could be detrimental in the future, should an employee reveal that they were forced to sign a document we knew to be illegal in CA. The VCs are still demanding that we make all employees, including ourselves sign, and we are now happily doing so in the knowledge we'll use this against the company if we need to. Just the kind of corporate loyalty you want to instill early on with your management and employees.

All the open issues are in Dick's court (excuse the pun) and we've been waiting for over a week for any kind of acknowledgement that he's looking at them. I've had to strong-arm our lead VC repeatedly to get a day or two's progress out of Dick, before he slips back into his old ways. It's time-consuming but more than that, it is emotionally draining; every day that passes brings us closer to having a zeroed bank balance again—something that I am painfully reminded of as I signed manual paychecks again today.

After three days (including the weekend) during which our lawyers were unable to even reach Dick to see if he was still alive, the associate finally reached him today. She asked him for status on the open issues, but he was evasive. She reminded him that he had promised to be done last week, and the week before for that matter. He denied, dissembled and lied as he was backed into the corner. Finally, the associate used the only stick that seemed to have worked in the past: "I'm just trying to avoid having to get my client to contact the VCs again and have them hammer you again."

"I don't have to listen to you, your client, or *my clients*; I'll give it to you when I feel like it," came the reply from Dick. Tears and laughter followed swiftly afterwards by me.

June 16th: "In the Valley"

Being in Silicon Valley is great—unless your investors aren't here too. The glut of companies that have raised millions of dollars and aren't afraid to spend it on grand offices in prestigious locations have been taught well by Valley venture capitalists who saw in the 1990s that it isn't what you do as a business but how brazenly you spend that gets you noticed and eventually underwritten for an IPO. So, with companies spending freely to secure space—and the equipment and people within it—for startups like us, crazily bucking this trend and trying to save money and operate economically is not easy. To have out-of-the-Valley VCs exacerbates this problem immeasurably. Every budgetary expense is questioned down to the penny. Not in itself a bad thing, and certainly to be expected if not commended by a good VC (well maybe not the penny-pinching part). Nevertheless, the cost of doing business in Silicon Valley is very different to that in Chicago or Washington, where our investors reside. Even when we've provided compensation surveys and real estate listings evidencing our budgetary projections, the investors balk at the cost of the operation. And to reiterate, we are prudent to the point of frugality in an atmosphere where squandering money is a badge of honor. Perhaps that's our problem; still I just can't justify spending on things that don't make us good, but only make us look good. Spending on the essentials, though, still requires paying a significant premium over the Valley-less area known as the rest of the country. We have begun to sound like a broken record as every budget-item justification begins with: "Well, in the Valley..."

Once again, I feel like alarm bells ought to be ringing alerting us to signs of future problems. Our investors have an ambivalent attitude towards Silicon Valley. On the one hand, there is their feeling of uncontrollable excess (justified to an extent) and that the Valley and its successful investment professionals really do not deserve the attention they get; on the other, their profound desire to be a part of the big game here coupled with an inferiority complex about being minor league VCs by not being in the Valley. Oftentimes our lead investor complains about Sand Hill Road (synonymous with successful venture capital and known as the "Wall Street of the West"), and in the same conversation talks about how he plans to open up a satellite office here. For our investors, denigrating the Valley and us for being here has repeatedly been a theme in closing our funding: it is almost a badge of honor for our VCs to reject any proposal or standard clause coming out of our Valley-based legal counsel. I'd like to believe this is simply a tough negotiating tactic—"the best deal you get is the one going in"; they play that line as often as we're saying: "But, in the Valley". I consider this fair as a tactic, and take the advice to heart too, making sure we get the best deal we can too. Of course, when you are the one with your hand out, "beggars can't be choosers" becomes more than an old chestnut.

The reality though is that us being in the Valley, and our investors not, is slowing down our funding close significantly. The legal wrangling between the eponymous Dick and our legal counsel is simply one example of how we have lost the huge benefit of the unspoken understanding between Valley lawyers, venture capitalists and entrepreneurs that allows standard Valley business practices to be accepted rather than endlessly debated with suspicion.

Our lawyers have asked us if we're certain we want to take capital from out-side-the-Valley VCs and be stuck with these investors for our foreseeable business life. I take these warnings seriously, but trust that once we close the funding, we'll all be on the same side, and the attacks and delays will end. After all, it would make no sense for our investors to be destroying their own multimillion-dollar investment—would it?

June 24th: Accounting Hell and the Paperwork Devil

Financial people in companies seem to me to come in a couple of sizes: the 'hustler' and the 'pit-bull'.

The hustler is looking for ways to extract dollars and aid the P&L through "creative" means: I just saw an election campaign story showing Dick Cheney—the Republican Vice-Presidential candidate—describing creativity as what Arthur Anderson's major benefit to his company Halliburton is. I'm not sure whether the story was suggesting this was smart or suspect. But manipulating numbers, bending accounting rules and other creative methods of increasing revenues or profits on paper if not necessarily in reality, have long been part of the financial game—the reason we need an accounting profession in the first place—and unfortunately, not well understood by the investing layperson that expects these figures to be carefully policed. For your average individual investor deciding between the thousands of companies they can put their money into, the only protection—a false protection in reality—is that the accounting firms are applying their creative techniques to all of those companies at the same time. Let's just hope they're not being *too* creative, or the whole market may be shaken as a result.

The pit-bull, on the other hand, is always looking to help the bottom-line by squeezing every budget dollar that little bit further. They tend to be a pain-in-the-ass to anyone trying to deal with them. And unfortunately tend to penny-pinch but not see the forest for the trees at times.

In spite of the difficulties dealing with the latter personality, I would personally rather work with the pit-bull than the hustler if I had to choose. With our lead investor, I certainly got my wish!

Iris (not her real name, but close enough to IRS in how fearsome and irritating she was) was a continuous thorn in my side, simply due to her ability to make the simplest task turn into endless document churn. On many occasions, I have been asked to provide a financial document, only to have it returned as Iris prefers some row as a column, or some number re-justified, more often in the document-formatting sense than the financial one.

I made the mistake of suggesting to Iris that she go ahead and reformat the spreadsheets to her liking, and was treated to a primer on accounting practices and the legal liability attached to anyone who touched the numbers or the formatting.

Having learned my lesson, I spent some time trying to deduce Iris's desired format, and a few iterations—and discoveries about Microsoft Excel—later, I now know the difference between Miscellaneous Expenditures and Miscellaneous Expenses.

While I understand the necessity of doing things accurately when it comes to corporate accounts, at some point, future projections simply become best guesses. Explaining the reasoning why our budget estimates for office supplies for June three years in the future has jumped by 5% per year (from $200 to $230) seems excessive: this is what Iris demanded I respond to today. The fact that the total amounts equal the wages 'wasted' as I spent my time documenting in detail how these figures were determined today, escapes Iris. Not that I mind making the projections, or validating them internally, but being required to provide written documentation of the reasoning stretches things a bit far. Iris insists that verbal explanations are insufficient; this specifically includes the verbal explanation I offered today: "I know you want a paper-trail so you can cover your ass—but no matter how big your ass is, I've sent you enough paper to cover it twice now."

There are a couple of key factors that I've found interesting working with our lawyers. First, there was the moment when we truly realized the difference between the corporation we now worked for and ourselves as founders. Our law firm is our corporate legal representative. It represents our company, not us as individuals or as founding employees. This means oftentimes I am reviewing documents beneficial to the corporation, but not so much for me as a founder or employee. I've attempted to take my role as a corporate officer very seriously in these cases, though it is tempting to avoid the harshest protections the company can handcuff us with. Luckily for the corporation, they have backup protection in our opposing counsel. In negotiating with our investors as we try to close our Series-A venture funding, there is clearly an established difference between us—the enemy—and the corporation—in their minds, an enemy of the enemy. This difference was not so apparent when it was just the three of us in a one-room office for all those months, but in forming a company to protect ourselves as individuals, the flipside is that the company wants to be protected from us at times too.

To our lawyers' credit, they have so far advised us in good faith: as management of the corporation, and in our founders' roles when requiring standard protections from both the corporation and the investors. Never offering advantages to us specifically—and maintaining at all cost their charter of representing the corporation—we have had several discussions on hypothetical founders of other (scarily similar) companies, who would do well to demand certain protections, or the removal of particularly harsh clauses.

The second, related factor in ploughing through all this documentation is how interconnected all these relationships and roles have become. I am a founder of the company; I am an employee of the company; I am in executive management of the company; I am a shareholder of the company; I am on the Board of Directors of the company; I am the corporate President. Depending on which legal documents we're negotiating, I sometimes wear one, two, three or more of these hats. Navigating this is something completely new to me and having lawyers to explain the nuances and balance each role when they conflict is essential. Most importantly, our legal counsel raise alarm bells and red flags as our investors—through their legal proxy—try to slip various suspect clauses past us, diminishing our protections or tipping the balance in their favor, typically to our detriment. On more than one occasion, we've confronted Dick with a suspiciously worded clause that he quickly refutes with a: "now how did that get in there?"

The amount of paperwork required to close a funding is copious. The lawyers, who of course are being paid to produce it, control how much of it is truly necessary and relevant. I am struck again by the beauty of the legal system: given these are the same parties that will be suing each other later over anything we missed, it seems mostly a game to see what you can slip by the other side up front. For the most part though, the key to racking up those billable hours is in endless tweaking of words and clauses in entirely meaningless ways: re-numbering and re-labeling lists of items from 1.a and 1.b to 1.i and 1.ii, for example. These kinds of manipulation require a redline comparison (named for the indications traditionally made with a red pen to edits in a hardcopy document); you have to make sure your eyes don't miss an extra "i" or "iii" that sneaks back in a previously rejected clause that offered up your first-born child to be the investors' limo driver. As I am unmarried with no children, I have less to fear than my cofounders, who often express concern that I might not be looking for "first-born child" clauses as closely as I should be. I retaliate by suggesting they read the hundreds of pages of documents themselves, at which point they defer to my superior ability to tolerate hours of investor bullshit.

The documentation process has drawn us closer as a team, building a great deal of trust on our side by necessity: from my partners to me, and from me to the lawyers; though at times—with all the legal rewording I am suggesting myself at this point—our senior associate says I might not need her assistance after all. I honestly tell her in response that recruiting the firm's services is singularly the best decision we have made thus far, and we'd be doomed without them. Given the pace of the funding process, I just hope we're not doomed regardless.

June 30th: Over Before We Begin

I told myself on starting the business to mentally record as much as possible of anything positive that happened, especially in the early days. I think any entrepreneur or small business owner knows the feeling of elation that comes from the early moments—when even the simplest tasks (like emptying out the trash out of all our offices—*our* offices!) seem enjoyable. It allows you to recall these moments in the dark days that will follow; and there are always dark days ahead, no matter how successful you are overall. I promised to take time to breathe it all in, despite being pulled in seventeen directions at all times and a growing recognition that there really are never enough hours in the day.

I've never run a business before, but it compares in a way to when I bought my first home; you find yourself just walking from room to room with a smile on your face, planning how you're going to decorate and modify, or just simply taking in the fact that it's all yours to control.

So yes, I am very glad I remembered all the early wonder…because I wonder now if that's going to be our entire—extremely short—history.

We have two weeks' money left after the payroll checks I handed out today clear the bank. March (when we successfully pitched to the investors) and April (when we finally received the termsheet setting out the millions we were to receive) seem a lifetime ago now. And it has indeed been a lifetime: a life in which I gave birth to a baby company, nurtured it with an office and employees to feed and clothe it, and now that it's ready to take its first step, I'm about to starve it to death.

Okay, so infanticide is perhaps a bit of an extreme analogy. Still, there is a sense that I'm losing my first-born child here, and it's a slow, agonizing death before my eyes.

We continue to be stuck simply on trivia and minutiae, and delayed by Dick's recalcitrance. The investors are the ones to hold accountable in reality though. I have come to realize that they have no interest in wiring us any more money until what we have in the bank is depleted. Every hold-up is simply a distraction meant to drive us to that date. I would spend the money more quickly—there are more than enough invoices stacking up to be paid—but I suspect the inability to keep to our declared budget for two months would not be a great opening gambit in the business-relationship chess game we appear to be playing here.

I have simply reverted to explaining that the employees are all out looking for other employment and I'm spending too many cycles convincing them that we are a viable business. The investors sound dubious, but do understand what two weeks' notice is, and in effect, that's what we've given here, since two weeks' funds are all we have left. Their demands for employee patience are hollow as I explain we exhausted our goodwill on that front back in April and May. Regardless of whether the employees trust more money is on the way, they do not relish the constant uncertainty, and more stable—and lucrative—positions may lure them away at any time. I think these portents of doom are having a slow effect: the osmosis of panic penetrating to the point that we are (finally?) clearing the last few issues daily now.

I have learned that the squeaky wheel most definitely gets the grease. My first assignment each morning is to put in calls and emails to both the investors, and a global "are we there yet" email to everyone I can think of, from lawyers to accountants to investors to the janitors and receptionist—everyone who has an email or voicemail I have access to.

My second task is to visit with our small band of employees and project an air of calm and optimism that belies our situation. I have decided though that I will not completely shelter my people from our status—now and in the future—regardless of the negative or positive. They don't need the details, but they deserve to be aware of our position. I have heard of too many companies where employees show up one day to find the building shuttered and some poor human resources sucker left to hold off the angry natives with an insufficient amount of ammo, in the form of envelopes containing employees' last paychecks—if they are lucky. More often that not, startup executives are simply emptying out the bank account making sure they are able to take a comfortable flight from their corporate responsibilities—a golden jetpack so to speak—while employees are stuck on the ground negotiating with angry, unpaid landlords just to get access to their personal belongings. In one of my former companies (after I was gone), I was told the employees were asked to drive U-Haul trucks in on a Saturday to clear out all the equipment and store it in their homes, as the rent wasn't going to be paid on the Monday, and the company anticipated the landlord locking them out and auctioning off whatever was inside—company-owned or not—as recompense.

These stories are common enough; I have felt in the dark personally in previous companies so I understand the effects on employees well. Typically, there are two groups in any company: the clueless, who are loyal company evangelists until the shocking end, when their entire fantasy bubble pops, and they are left extremely bitter at those they trusted; the clued-in are those who are closer to management decisions or can see the signs indirectly from the movements and reports of customers, sales, or 'the numbers'. The clued-in tend to exhibit a subdued bitterness throughout the company's demise, particularly if management does not acknowledge its imminence to the employee pool as a whole; I can attest to this as one of the clued-in at my previous company.

In either case, the bitterness is not caused by the loss of employment or downfall of the company, but by the attitude of management and executives that employees are incapable of being trusted with such grown-up information. In a position of corporate guardianship, taking care of the needs of employees, management often begins treating employees like children.

One management assumption is often that employees will leave at the first sign of trouble. Certainly the employment climate at the given time affects this, but in my experience this viewpoint gives far too little credit to workers. Employees are far more loyal to their employers than the reverse. Part of this is simply corporate necessity: a business employs people to make money, not just for the sake of giving them a livelihood. The problem too often lies in the attitudes exhibited by many executives towards employees. At too many corporations, large and small, management creates an antagonistic "us versus them" attitude towards employees. This causes far greater disruption when the chips are down than would be the case if the standard operating procedure were more congenial and respectful.

I believe keeping the employees aware of the potential for future quakes—while not spreading panic at minor tremors—offers them a greater sense of ownership in our enterprise, and in the end will keep us together, longer, in tough times. I'd hope for such treatment myself as an employee—I can hardly deny it to others now I have the chance.

July 6th: We are Officially a Joke at the Bar

We are famous. Actually, we are infamous. Our lawyers told us today that the never-ending story of our funding has become a cautionary tale taught to law firms around the Valley. We have been unofficially named the "worst funding close ever". Unofficially, because we haven't actually closed yet, so we may end up being the "worst funding close never" as our senior associate sardonically put it.

For anyone thinking of doing business with outside-the-Valley venture capitalists or law firms (excluding New York's financial center which shares the Valley's work ethic these days), we have become the exemplar for why you want to run the other way. Our investors and their legal representation have become myth and legend—"Here be Dragons!"

I'm tempted to let our investors know this, but I doubt they'd take it with the same resigned humor that I did.

What is particularly strange is—at first glance—our funding is not taking an abnormally long time. Most entrepreneurs I've spoken with say it's a three-month process to close a first funding round after receiving a termsheet; we'll be hitting that in about ten days, just as we also run out of money. Our problem lies in why we're taking this long, and what we're arguing over.

For our investors, their primary goal of course is to maximize the money they make on their investment; any smart investor would be expected to operate on this basis. This has been reflected in them fighting hard to make clauses more favorable to them than to founders, employees or future investors, and I do not consider this unreasonable, or believe any astute investor would do otherwise. The trouble lies beyond this, in that their goal also seems to be to undercut clauses that do not affect them, but in any way benefit employees or founders. This concerns me for the long-term: I recognize how this could negatively frame everything ahead of us, should the investors feel their interests diverge from ours or that of the corporation. My focus in funding negotiations has tended to be towards the good of the company and what is best to get it running and then keep it running. Secondary in my mind has been how I will best come out of it. Not altruistically, but with a belief that a successful company will lead to achieving my personal goals, professional and financial. In contrast, we do not seem to have investors seeking equitable agreements where everyone can prosper, but already seeking to secure the largest portion of a small pot, as opposed to working together to make the pot greater for all.

One key lesson I have learned is that you have to become an informal but informed legal expert yourself. Particularly because this is a process where the experts make more money the longer the process lasts. I have spent ten hours a day, seven days a week, for almost three months reading thousands of pages of legal documents. It has been the smallest clauses that have caused the greatest problems. Being able to suggest language and argue the finer points of a clause with investors or lawyers is akin to taking your car to the garage and not being duped by a mechanic. If you don't know a convertible-note from a ratcheting-down clause, you can get your driveshaft shoved up your head-gasket, so to speak.

The reasons behind our delays beyond the expected negotiations are what have truly made us a cause célèbre for lawyers in Palo Alto—a city with the highest concentration of lawyers per capita in the country, and thus making us the talk of local Bar and local bars alike.

Dick's unprofessionalism; our investors' strange insistence on illegal clauses; the repeated preemptive "we don't like it" proclamations on any suggestion our lawyers offer: whether it's to accelerate the process, or to make us more attractive to future investors by incorporating standard Valley-terms and structures, thereby saving us money or making us more valuable—characteristics you'd expect an investor to embrace. All have been weaved into a scary bedtime story lawyers are now reading to their demonic offspring as they tuck them in at night.

July 13th: We are Done! No Wait...

Charlie Brown has nothing on us. Our investors—hereafter known as Lucy Van Pelt—have yanked the funding football away from our swinging foot one more time.

I seem to keep writing this: we are done…no, wait…there is one more thing that has come up. This time, it is to do with the "founders' representations". A small document that we, as founders, have to sign off on, that personally holds us accountable for the state of the company prior to the funding close. Not a problem, other than what any misrepresentation might mean: both in terms of description and consequences.

A misrepresentation can mean anything incorrect, even if we believe it's correct right now. That is something I could not agree to, and we've been battling for two days now on acceptable wording that protects the investors—a legitimate requirement—and still allows us to actually make good faith representations. The investors seem to understand my point, but that isn't moving them towards incorporating it.

An example of a potential misrepresentation is our belief that our technology will be patentable, and there's nothing being patented already that might conflict with it. As far as we know, this would be a true statement, but early stage patent applications are not public, so if someone sent their application out yesterday, we're not going to be aware of it for a while. Some sort of "good faith" wording is going to get in there, but it is tiresome having to argue this point for more than five minutes—it's been more like three days at this point. I have resorted to simply saying if the investors have zero trust in us, they shouldn't be investing. A dangerous suggestion to make; but they know it's posturing on my part and have taken it as me "over-dramatically making my point" as our secondary VC said this morning. "If I'm making my point," I said, "I'll be as over-dramatic as I have to be."

The consequences are where our greater concerns lie. We are personally liable to make amends if there's a misrepresentation of the corporation's standing. We do not want to be in a position of putting our homes and bank accounts on the line, or having to pay out large sums of money that have been used legitimately to build the business. (One suggestion was that we personally have to pay back the two hundred thousand dollars already invested.)

I am not sure how we can reach a compromise on what is essentially a no-compromise issue for my co-founders. Personally, I am willing to 'rep' to specifics, as long as the focus is narrow and clear, and the investors agree to all representations being in good faith based on facts known at the time we sign. It is painful to have to bring both sides closer together on this last issue; usually, I've been able to simply present the founders' position and draw the investors towards it as much as possible. Here, for the first time, I have to move my colleagues and myself as much as the VCs; not a happy circumstance to be in so early on, regardless of whether I can rationalize it from the investors' point of view.

I've spent months compromising with our VCs, but this is the first time compromising our own principles.

July 14th: VCs Don't Wire on Fridays

Everything was complete. All set to go. Millions of dollars on the way—imminently! And then I realized it was a Friday. VCs don't wire funds on a Friday. It's a curious rule, but one I've now heard enough times to confirm our own anecdotal evidence is correct.

As a startup, the weekend just means you have two more days a week to work. For folks with a financial background, I guess market hours restrict their thinking. So you don't get money on a Friday, because you're presumably not working on Saturday to need the money. Maybe it's that, maybe it's the extra few dollars of interest earned holding onto the money. Either way, it means we're not getting funded today, tomorrow or Sunday.

The fun part is that yet again, I have to modify all the documents to reflect a new closing date. We also give up just a few more shares in interest on our bridge loans. Worse though, I get to spend another weekend wondering if we're really done, or if some new, mysterious quibble, or clause will push the date back yet again.

We reached finality on everything. Good faith representations, with a narrow focus on currently known facts, and only willful malfeasance incurring penalties. Salaries, benefits, budgets, employee contracts, everything done to the satisfaction of the investors, and usually to a mild dissatisfaction from our lawyers and grudging resignation by me. We were just one day too late finishing…and now it's Friday.

The best part of my day was writing everyone's paycheck. Everyone's last paycheck, if we aren't done with the funding. I feel like a broken record, repeating this every two weeks, but at least this time, I know there's no money left in the bank account, so I won't be saying it again.

"Go have fun this weekend," said our lead investor breezily. "The real hard work begins on Monday with your funded company."

I hope so, I really do.

July 17th: Third Time's a Charm

Today (it's hard to even write this for fear I'm somehow going to jinx it even though it's already done) we closed our first round of funding. I have had two competing emotions all day: excitement and relief, with the latter winning out handily. We finally saw millions of dollars flow into our bank account this morning; a number with six zeroes after it on your bank statement is quite thrilling!

It has been a long time coming, which should perhaps make it all the sweeter, but instead the process has simply left me drained and concerned about our future relationship with our investors. The delays in funding may not have cost us in time (we are after all a nascent technology aiming to meet a future market demand that will become apparent in two to three years); but it has cost a great deal in our energy and optimism. An abstract cost certainly, but one that substantively slows our progress. I myself feel the need to mentally coast for a while, though I know it's impossible to do so, given the long list of neglected business development tasks I need to catch up on, as I've been wasting my time negotiating funding terms.

There is this brief pause for breath now that we have funding, but I must almost immediately begin to think about ways to bring in additional funds into the company. To do that, we must make enough progress as a business to warrant a new investment at an increased valuation. Everything is interconnected: we raised this money to build our business to the next level, so in turn we can raise more funding to take us to the next level, so in turn that can build the business to the point we can stand alone on our revenues or—as many a Dotcom has dreamed of—we take the company public.

Every decision we make now thus affects our potential future. It's dizzying to contemplate, and so I choose not to; for the next few weeks, tactical positioning is more important than long-term strategy.

Tactics include hiring a development team as quickly as we can, and marketing our brand to the world—even if there is nothing behind that brand for now.

Branding is something I am good at. It's easy to understand, and for most products and companies in the world today, branding is the fundamental key to success. Far more vital than products or services, branding hides, unseen in the background, driving us to buy particular products or services whether they are better than the competition or not.

It's not that a good product is unnecessary, but it is that a good (even great) product is not sufficient. Positioning the product—or more accurately the brand—determines its success in the marketplace, and your company's success too as a result.

The McDonald's 'Golden Arches' are the most recognizable brand in the world. If you're asked to think about cola, Coke might be the first one you think of, but is it the taste or the brand identity guiding your thoughts? Some brands, like Coke, Hoover (vacuum cleaner), Kleenex (tissues) or Tupperware (containers), have become synonymous with the products they sell. That is successful branding! There are over a dozen brands of cola on the market (not counting supermarket generics) and yet Coke is what most people ask for.

Before we have our product built, we need to establish ourselves through a brand identity that intrigues people enough to want to know what they can spend money on that has the brand attached. The trick of course is to have a product actually available by the time the brand is hot.

Now that we have some money, branding becomes possible, but we still have to undertake a guerilla-marketing campaign to accomplish our goals. Our entire first-round of funding is less than the weekly marketing budget for an industry heavyweight. Still, I have taken on the 800lb gorillas in a market before and been successful—guerilla beats gorilla if you're smart about it.

When you are small, the important thing is to have help promoting your brand, and that means creating a community that will evangelize you. If you do it right, your followers will be far more vociferous in your support than even you can be. The added advantage being that external promotion of your brand is far superior to doing it yourself: people trust third parties raving about you far more than any advertising campaign you can put together yourself.

We have a great marketing team and a solid marketing plan ready to go, and now we have the budget to execute it. On the engineering side, we need a lot more warm bodies and quickly.

So for a moment—just a moment—I can relax into the relief of knowing I have gotten the company going…deep breath…sigh…

Now that the moment is over, it is time to look forward: I have the company up; now I need to keep it running.

End of Part One

PART TWO: Running

July 27th: Hiring in a Recession

We are in a local recession. The market is in freefall. The Dotcoms have disintegrated faster than the Alka-Seltzer in a venture capitalist's drinking water. The Valley is in turmoil. We have funding and we are hiring. This should have been a great fit.

Unfortunately, no one really believes it's all over yet. Venture capitalists, institutional investors and the stock-buying public have been left shell-shocked by the market collapse and end of the IPO pipeline, but they continue to nurse hopes of a comeback or one last big win that will recapture some or all of their losses or at least some lost glory. In the same way, workers have not absorbed what the correction means to the employment market.

Today we interviewed a 'young stud' as I've come to refer to them. These are fresh-out-of-college software engineers (with an undergrad degree in Computer Science or Electrical Engineering) who maybe have a year's professional experience and have only known an up-market until now. As a result, they believe that the salaries and benefits (including some of the ludicrous perks that had been offered) to employees are standard fare, and not the product of a booming market and the difficulties of hiring and retaining qualified personnel in the late 1990s.

In my view, many cost-effective employee benefits offer tremendous gains to the corporation. For example, offering free dinners (as many Silicon Valley companies did in the 1990s) was a terrific perk to employees. It was just as terrific certainly as a cost-effective productivity tool. Giving a highly skilled software engineer salaried at fifty dollars an hour a twenty-dollar dinner to get two extra hours of work per night was a bargain. "A happy employee is a productive employee," as Mr. Burns from the cartoon The Simpsons once said.

Even well reported-on referral bonuses such as giving a Ferrari sports car to an employee if they recommended and brought-in ten qualified new personnel actually made financial sense. Given professional recruiters would typically take twenty to thirty thousand dollar fees per employee they placed with a firm, hiring ten new workers could cost two to three hundred thousand dollars in total. The

Ferrari would cost less than that, and you'd get an extremely happy employee to boot. (At least until they realized the monthly cost of insuring the car would take more than half their paycheck.)

An entire workforce would be bringing in personally vetted quality candidates; but there were a couple of downsides. You might have employees spending more time on recruiting than on doing their jobs; and the lure of a Ferrari might make them less discretionary in the qualification of their referrals. Both these problems were things I saw in my previous company, and that was without the Ferrari, merely twenty-five hundred dollars per hired candidate. Some employees were making more bringing in candidates than they were in salary. Not that the candidates were all bad—but they weren't all good, or even all qualified either.

All of this: the difficulties of hiring; the cost of recruiting good candidates; and younger workers not knowing what a down job-market looked like, allowed me to humor the young stud as he sat before me, listing his demands. He wanted a hundred and forty thousand dollars a year. That was the part that threw me. The rest of the demands about vacations, benefits and perks were amusing too, but the salary was what really got me. I looked at his résumé again, just to be sure I wasn't missing something: he had six months' work experience after completing his Bachelor's Degree.

This was a junior position, I explained to him. He didn't consider himself a junior engineer, despite his lack of experience. I admired his self-belief, then tried the tack of describing our startup situation, and how we were early-stage, without large funding, but he would have higher potential rewards upon our success for being here early. Stud stuck to his guns, offering to perhaps drop a week off of his four-week annual vacation demands. I appreciated his offer, given this was putting him back in line with the rest of the company, but again explained that he'd need to also take at least a fifty thousand a year pay-cut and would still be being ridiculously compensated given his experience.

We parted company, with Stud casually mentioning that he did have another offer at his inflated salary with another startup, and that we had no chance of hiring good engineers based on what we were willing to pay. I told him if someone was offering him that much money, he should be banging on their door, and not shopping for other offers, and in fact, I wouldn't mind going to work for this company since I'd be getting a pay-raise too. However, I warned him that a startup crazy enough to be paying such huge salaries to junior staff would not likely last too long, as they clearly had no idea how to manage their funds. He left with a grin that I interpreted as a smirk at my cluelessness. I let him leave knowing the grin will be wiped off his face in the near future, one way or another.

I sure hope the recession hits the job market soon. We're in sorry need of a correction that will remind workers that it wasn't always all about massages and personal concierges; and that there's no such thing as a free dinner—or lunch—anymore.

August 14th: Bored Meeting

Today was our first board meeting. The investors flew in for the day, to see our new building, meet the team and talk about the future. Of course, our lead investor didn't show up on time. So our 10am meeting became an informal meet-and-greet with our secondary VC (who showed up an hour early—glad I told everyone to be in the office even earlier today!). Having waited until noon, we decided to head for lunch when we finally heard from the lead; he said he'd join us at lunch and we could have the official board meeting afterwards.

Lunch was good—the investors were paying, so they picked an expensive restaurant. We've been going to the coffee shop around the corner to grab a sandwich or pastry—when we've had time to eat lunch at all—so this was a rare treat. We've often marveled at the fun life a venture capitalist must have: they get to listen to cool ideas every day, dismiss the ones they don't like, and steal the ones they do for existing portfolio companies, or wield excessive powers over an entrepreneur even if they do plan to invest. Throughout, they get to meet in fancy restaurants, often jetting around the country, and stay in nice hotels. It's not for everyone, but I can think of worse things to do every day. Of course, they also need some of those investments to make money, so they can provide a good return to their own institutional investors. When most venture capitalists are shooting for one out of ten of their investments to make it big though, the odds are in their favor that blind luck—or an over-excited Wall Street—will take care of them.

Having eaten and made merry (even I was forced to put aside my resentment at the last few months of torture and enjoy the new camaraderie we now shared as fellow shareholders), we headed back to go through our first official board meeting as a funded company. Sure, we had board meetings before, but Jay, Al and me in our executive suite discussing a corporation that only existed on paper for the most part, didn't have the same sense of formality.

I had prepared an agenda, which I hoped passed muster. It seemed to, but only because we never really stuck to it. Our lead investor spent most of the time on his cellphone. It turns out he was flying out this evening, so we only had him for a couple of hours after lunch, and he spent about ninety-five minutes of that on his phone. Our secondary investor looked as exasperated as we did, but his suggestion that the lead switch off his phone for a while to not be interrupted was ignored.

We did get a few items out of the way, including approving our stock option plan and discount options for our first employees. We also got employee benefits formally endorsed, even though we had gone ahead and enrolled folks before-hand. There are a lot of formalities behind a corporation, and one was going to be the requirement that I submitted detailed financials on a monthly basis. "No problem" I said, as a nagging voice in my head, sounding a lot like Iris was com-plaining about my Excel document formatting skills again.

The rest of the meeting passed smoothly. I had been nervous about how things would go, but we're all just happy to be getting on with the job of moving the company forward, and—interruptions by that damn cellphone notwithstand-ing—I actually have far greater confidence that this is all going to work. The investors are looking forward to our future success, and for the first time in a while, I can't say I disagree with them.

September 3rd: Size Matters!

We are small. A couple of million times bigger than we were a couple of months ago, but compared to the elephantine companies we are trying to do business with, we are a tiny mouse.

Getting the attention of an elephant when you are a mouse is difficult, but not impossible. My memory of cartoons suggests that once you have their attention, they react pretty strongly, and that's what we're banking on as we run around trying to catch their eye, while avoiding being trampled by oblivious limbs.

Making yourself seem bigger is all about marketing and alliances. Well-placed advertising, the aforementioned branding, and being promoted in the right media make you seem like you are a big player in your industry. This is one reason why the Dotcoms spent so much cash so fast. Advertising rates on a single billboard in the Bay Area during the late 1990s boom could be over a million dollars a year. One billboard. Taking out monthly full-page ads in magazines like *Red Herring* or *Fortune* would add many more millions in annual marketing budgets too. The old adage: "you have to spend money to make money" became: "you have to spend venture money to raise more venture money"; companies were spending what they raised simply to attract more investment—not on creating a real business, but in promoting themselves as the next big thing that you had to get your money into immediately; before the train left the station; before the general populous realized how great the company was.

Advertising was a self-fulfilling market too for many Internet businesses. Their entire business plan was predicated on whatever they were doing driving people to visit a website on which they would sell advertising space. The greater the number of visitors (or "eyeballs" as they're known in the industry) you had visiting your website, the more you could charge for advertising space. It didn't matter what was on the site, only whether people would visit it or not.

With no emphasis on product or service, simply on promotion, success was down to how well you could advertise your site and your company brand. Buying advertising space on other popular websites was one way; they would similarly buy advertising space on your site too. No money would actually change hands, but you could both show advertising revenue on your books. Another brilliant accounting scheme, but in the end, you weren't actually making any of the only thing that matters: money.

The market collapse was inevitable due to the symbiotic nature of Internet companies. If a big player ran out of money, they were no longer spending their millions on advertising. Those millions, which had gone to other Internet companies along with new media companies, disappeared, making these Internet and media companies begin to collapse, and their advertising dollars, spent on yet more Internet and media companies, dried up, causing a cascade effect.

For the infrastructure providers (like Sun Microsystems, Oracle Corp, Cisco, or Intel), who sold the hardware and software to operate these companies, the collapse was also dramatic. Not only were the big customers they had been supplying dropping like flies, but there was so much cheap equipment available in bankruptcy sales that any new companies seeking hardware or software no longer needed to purchase new products, they could just pick up existing infrastructure by bidding pennies on the dollar at clearance auctions.

With no market for new, next-generation, infrastructure products, the hardware and software manufacturers' sales and revenues are plummeting and they in turn are forced to layoff workers and skip an entire product cycle, essentially delaying by two or three years, the release of their next product version. They can only hope that things will recover by the time the second new product cycle comes along, but meanwhile, the whole technology industry will effectively slip back about three years.

All this means to us is that marketing has been stressed over a good product or service, and while there are many empty billboards on the sides of the major Valley highways, advertising is still too expensive a proposition for a small startup like us.

The way to increase your marketing and advertising budgets is through that second factor: alliances. By allying with bigger companies and organizations, we can leverage their deeper pockets to promote themselves and us along with them.

Co-marketing is something I've worked on a lot in the past, and—as long as you're really bringing some value to the bigger partner—it can be a real win-win situation for both parties. By bringing in technology, a brand or customer demographic that the big guy isn't reaching successfully on their own, you can slap your own name on the advertising they are paying for, or at least subsidizing for you. Co-marketing is not just limited to small companies; it's used successfully by the big guns too. Whether it's Intel having their little "Intel Inside" bumper at the end of all PC manufacturers' ads, or your Big Mac Meal coming with a Disney toy or Star Wars collector's cup, associating yourself with other successful brands and companies—and with big advertising budgets—is a winning strategy.

Our first alliance is with an organization formed from some of the bigger players in the technology industry who are venturing into our specific arena. As charter members of this organization, we get the benefits of being promoted by this forum and the gravitas that comes with being founders of a group steering the technology for the future. We also get a handy contact-list for each big company we need to be pitching to in the future, when we have a product to sell.

For now though, we're not looking to do much steering; we're quite content to be sitting in the backseat of the limo, being driven to the party with all the big-wigs sitting next to us.

September 16th: Enron

"Our lead investor has a friend."

My partners expressed surprise at this declaration as I pulled them into my office to give them a heads-up on what was going on this morning.

"I mean a *VC* friend," I continued, explaining away the possibility that he had the real kind, "and this friend wants to invest in us—probably around a half million dollars."

We have to make a big decision quickly: should we pursue this extra money now that we have cash in the bank? Should I spend what is likely to be another month of reopening our funding round and accommodating this new investor? Half a million dollars is a significant amount of money, but do we really need it now? Do we really need the extra stock dilution we'll all take? There are plenty of reasons not to do it.

"The VC firm is an arm of a big energy company," I said, "but from what I know about them, they are moving into other areas aggressively, and they are one of the biggest and fastest growing companies in the Fortune Top Ten. I'm sure you've heard of them. They're called Enron."

Both Jay and Al were familiar with the company being a rising star of US financial markets and its ties to one of the Presidential candidates. This was a significant 'pro' to the 'cons' we had thought of. Enron has deep pockets. While half a million isn't a lot right now, they will certainly be in a position to add to that in later rounds. They also have connections to big money and big customers that we could leverage to our benefit. If they are looking at our industry as a future growth area, it could mean they might just acquire us, or our technology, later on, and we could even shift our efforts to making us as attractive as possible for just such an acquisition.

I've heard some negative reports about the company itself; I called a friend in the energy industry earlier, who worked closely on some trading products with them; he describes them as snakes who had licensed his company's technology simply to understand it well enough to rip it off later.

Since I've just spent the last three months snake charming, another serpent in the mix is almost expected; whether it is due to his VC nature, or taking after his Enron corporate masters. As this is their venture arm, not the company itself, we'll be shielded from what sounds like routine corporate espionage shenanigans. We won't be doing business with them (yet), just taking their money to build what we are planning to anyway. If they want us to focus on projects for them, they will be paying customers just like everyone else. In fact, they'll be our first paying customers, which is not a bad thing in of itself. Besides, it would make little sense for them to steal our technology if they part-owned us as investors, and likely cheaper to just buy us out if they wanted our solution without us. For now, it is our expertise they are investing in, so I don't see us getting booted out anytime soon and I did a good job negotiating protections for us if someone does try to turf us out of our own company while buying the enterprise. It would be quite profitable personally so it's an acceptable risk. This is really getting ahead of ourselves though; regardless, I'm not too worried about such scenarios, as big businesses like Enron should know better than to endanger their reputations on small-fry, with such schemes.

My real fear is that opening up our funding round again is going to lead to renegotiating all those clauses we haggled over the first time around. Seeking our lawyers' advice, they compared our funding round to "a can of worms" and "Pandora's box" when I asked about opening it up again. I seem to recall phrases like "are you nuts" and "you're kidding, right?" being thrown around too.

On balance, we have decided to open "exploratory discussions" with Enron, and if things look good, we'll actually start the process of redoing our Series A Funding to accommodate a new investor and board member.

The lawyers convinced us with the following argument: a bigger, established venture fund like Enron's might actually make long term sense since it will temper the extremes of our current lead VC.

Assuming Enron's venture arm is not as evil as my friend reports the corporation is; are not as evil as most venture capitalists; and are not as evil as I imagine any friend of our lead investor has to be; we'll be bringing into our investor cabal a sense of professionalism that a company like Enron presumably has in order to be successful. It's about time.

October 27th: A VC Buddy: Business Plan Blues

In their infinite wisdom, our investors have decided we need some assistance in producing a forward-looking business plan now that we are funded. This will be to start preparing for our next funding round, which we anticipate in about eighteen months. Our lead investor suggested we bring in a buddy of his based in Chicago as a consultant—and made it clear this wasn't a suggestion we could ignore.

"Buddy" seems a decent enough guy: he's smart, personable and has an MBA and some experience in management consultancy. This also means he doesn't come cheap. We have been ordered to pay him two thousand dollars a week, plus expenses, along with a bonus on completion of his efforts. He's expected to be with us for a month, so we're looking at ten to fifteen thousand dollars of cost. If he can deliver though, I guess I can live with his fees. That is still an open question though.

Buddy has been with us for almost a week now, and has decided that he'd like to spend his weekends in Chicago—at our expense of course—so he plans on flying away every Friday, and coming back in on a Monday morning. Beyond the expense of doing this, it also means we're only getting him for three full days a week, and suddenly that two thousand dollar weekly stipend seems a lot pricier. I think we might need to put a stop to this, but what surprises me is how freely he suggested this arrangement with an expectation of acquiescence on my part. He looked shocked when I began listing the reasons I didn't like the idea; like a spoiled child who had been rebuked by a neighbor and looked like he needed to run back to his venture mommy for a hug. Needless to say, I got a call from our lead investor soon after suggesting that Buddy could do lots of work for us on the plane, flying to and from Chicago.

My main concern is the lack of knowledge of our industry or of technology (not just ours—any technology), meaning I've had to spend a great deal of time educating him on our business, in order for him to write a business plan about it. The initial reasoning for him to be here was that I should be spending my time building the business rather than wasting time on refining our business plan; if only I was doing that instead of wasting more time explaining our market to a layman.

I have accepted Buddy's presence both as a test of our willingness to consent to investor input and of our investor seeking a greater comfort level with their own man in the mix early on. I don't have an MBA and this is the first company I'm running; even if he's taking advantage of his friendship to our VC to push his luck and expense account to the limit, I'm willing to have another good business brain join the trust and offer feedback and suggestions. I figure I may as well take advantage of the opportunity to pick Buddy's brain while he's picking my pocket.

November 17th: Viva Las Vegas

I'm sitting in a suite at the Venetian Hotel in Las Vegas as I write this. We just had a second great day at the Fall COMDEX Show, one of the big technology events of the year.

Yesterday we received a lot of interest in our solution, including being interviewed by the Show Daily—the newspaper passed out each morning to all attendees. Our article was in there this morning, just in time for the Board Meeting we had with our investors. They were also able to see our solution in action, as we demoed a prototype in our hotel room to a major strategic-partnership target. As the VCs looked on appreciatively, we ran a perfect demo, impressing enough to land a follow-up meeting with decision-makers after the show. The investors' confidence in our professional abilities has soared today, without a doubt.

It could of course have been a complete disaster; it seems all big shows are like that for technology companies. We were up through the night two straight days before we arrived here, still trying to get the demo to work. Yesterday we had a minor emergency when some of the software died, and we had to wipe everything clean and get a new version from the engineers sitting back in California. They are on standby in shifts, alternating catching up on lost sleep with manning the phones and computers at the office waiting for an SOS-call we thankfully didn't need to make today. If potential customers, the Press and our venture capitalists saw what it took to get a smooth prototype running flawlessly, they might be inclined to wonder if we have any idea what we're doing; still, I've worked in other companies where there's smoke and mirrors and little else in their demos. At least we have a real product, even if it's in skeletal form right now. We'll put meat on those bones soon enough.

This is our first open show, and we also chose this moment to go public with news of our funding and our company's existence. We decided to give ourselves some time to have something to show and talk about, before the coming-out party. Sending out a press release reporting our funding back in July would have been a waste—lost in the late summer vacation spell and with no event associated that we could leverage.

Instead, our press releases went out a couple of days before the show here, and we immediately got responses from interested parties looking to meet with us in Vegas: exactly as we planned. So far, we've gotten great exposure and everything has gone well. Our marketing department is small (numbering two people), but they are both brilliant at what they do.

Thankfully our Board Meeting (usually a dragged out snooze-fest) only lasted about twenty minutes. We had so much interest from COMDEX attendees that we couldn't spare a block of time that would exclude them from the demo-suite. It was more of a backslapping session, with a few formalities: approving previous minutes and an agenda, and the Board voting approval (in retrospect) on the press releases we put out (one of the VCs' requirements is to approve everything for now).

To allow more time for discussion (or more accurately, more time for us to listen to the VCs remind us about how wonderful they are), we did go to dinner tonight at what was an extremely upscale (i.e. expensive) Italian restaurant. All mahogany and leather. The wine the VCs ordered matched well with the opulence of the surroundings, and the bottles most certainly helped pay for the lavishness around us.

Fun though it was (even listening to the VCs was entertaining tonight), I would have enjoyed it all the more if I didn't know we were eventually going to foot the bill for the whole thing. This was one of the fun discoveries we made after our first Board Meeting and fancy lunch, which cost us several hundred bucks. That would've covered a couple of months of the Friday group-lunch we offered our half dozen employees weekly; I'd much rather have the money go to the people actually doing the work needed to make us an attractive business to investors…so we can take more investors out on expensive lunches in the future.

Tonight's bill—for the five of us (two investors and three founders)—was eleven hundred dollars. Anytime I spend money now, I inevitably compare the cost to all the other things I could use that money for, especially benefiting the employees in some way.

We recently instituted a monthly massage at the office. A masseuse would come in for three hours, and give everyone a half hour's back-and-shoulder therapy. It helped relieve stress and tension, especially with programmers hunched over keyboards and monitors all day. The cost was about three hundred dollars a session, but the value to the employees was immeasurable. So this dinner was three months of employee-massages. Or a year's office supplies. Or about fifteen hundred sugar-caffeine spiked sodas for engineers pulling all-nighters.

Okay, I'm even annoying myself with my constant moaning about money now—strangely I'm no miser with my personal funds but I'm a Scottish stereotype when it comes to penny-pinching with corporate cash.

Best not to dwell on the bills, and just enjoy celebrating the great day we've had. Everyone is in good spirits: we're off to a great start here with our big coming out party.

It's 2am and the casino beckons. Blackjack here I come. I wonder if I could double our funding on one hand at the tables?

January 8th: Jobs to India

We've been having a hard time hiring qualified employees; especially given the reasonable amount of money we're willing to offer totally unreasonable engineers and recruiters here.

So we've decided to employ a company in India to take part of our solution and develop it overseas. The cost benefit is incredible: an engineer in India costs us about 25% of an equivalent one here in the United States.

In our case though, it's not the cost benefit, but the warm bodies that are driving our decision. Our choice is to have the work done abroad, or not done at all. We picked the former without hesitation.

My only worry is how to manage the development process. It's difficult enough minding consultants and contractors when they are local, or at least within the same hemisphere. Eight thousand miles and thirteen time zones make it all the harder. Jay has taken responsibility (as the VP of Engineering, it is his responsibility, but I made him accept this task explicitly so everyone is clear who the go-to-guy is). I was the first point of contact with the contracting company, and they have a tendency to try to leap-frog Jay to make me the decision-maker, and that already has my alarm-bells ringing that managing the relationship is going to be harder than we think.

The contracting firm does look like a great proposition though. We are working with nascent technologies, and this firm claims expertise in many of the protocols we have to deal with. Finding qualified candidates has been difficult in the Valley, and we were surprised to discover groups of them half a world away. A little voice is telling me to be careful we're not being oversold, but we're trying to solidify expectations by making these guys deliver us an early beta version of the software; they have given us an aggressive date that will put us months ahead of schedule and below budget on this project. We still have several months of early design work that will be required before we're going to know for sure if this was a good idea, but for now, we just can't pass up the opportunity.

My view on off-shoring (or outsourcing) jobs is still mixed. I would prefer to hire local workers if only because management is so much easier. But we're going to be able to bring on a dozen Indian engineers for the cost of the two or three non-existent ones we can't hire here. I have a feeling that if the economy keeps going south the way it has been, we'll be able to fill those positions in a year or so, and the plan right now is to simply kick-start our development in India, and then bring it back in-house once we have the funds and the candidates available.

My concern is that when the time comes to bring the work back to the United States, it's hard for us to justify the cost increases to our investors—or to ourselves.

March 14th: VC Buddy #2: The French Connection

We are heading to France! It could be a major coup if we get a deal or some funding out of this trip. Somehow though, we have gotten another VC Buddy for our troubles. First, some background information to remind myself why this trip mattered so much.

One of the market realities we have had to deal with in our industry is that Europe and Asia are well ahead of the United States in terms of technology. While this means we struggle at times explaining the "future" to Americans, in Europe we are able to describe our products and generate considerable interest and excitement.

We have been able to generate a series of discussions with Vivendi, the erstwhile French conglomerate. Vivendi has risen from being a water-provider based in Paris, to holdings including entertainment (through their ownership of Universal), telecommunications (through France Telecom and stakes in many other national providers) and a multitude of other interests.

Vivendi's entertainment and multimedia holdings, tied with a mobile delivery system in Europe and beyond, are very exciting to us. Offering compelling content and a pipeline to deliver it to consumers makes Vivendi a potential dominator of our nascent industry, assuming they can overcome the crippling debt they have (mis-)managed themselves into. Vivendi-Universal can be compared to AOL-Time Warner: another vaunted merger of content and delivery system. Time (the non-magazine kind) will tell if combining compelling content and the access to it will be as accessible and compelling a business proposition to investors and the financial markets.

After some virtual "meet-and-greet" via email and phone over the past several months, we have done enough to earn ourselves a meeting in Paris to pitch our system for deployment in Europe. What we are really seeking though is an investment from Vivendi that will launch our Series-B funding round.

With finances tight as always, we are utilizing our two-founder strategy for the trip. I will attend as the business contact, and Jay will represent the technical aspects of the system and its deployment.

We broke the positive news to our investors about the trip a couple of weeks ago, as we worked towards nailing down a solid date. Our lead investor was excited. Not so much by our progress, but by the thought of Paris. He immediately offered to join us to demonstrate we were a real company with solid backing from our investors.

Having an investor sit in a meeting with customers is usually a positive. For small startups trying to do business with a billion-plus market cap multinational, you are always up against an impression of insignificance and impermanence. An investor in the room shows you will be around to deploy and support whatever you sell in future years.

We were delighted at the prospect of a productive meeting in Paris. Having an investor there also helped because you could have them ask the awkward questions about how much money Vivendi would be investing and when to expect the check. The heat for doing this would fall on our VC and not us, and we could even look bemused at the forwardness of it all, while still anticipating the answer eagerly.

Flights were booked, and we found as cheap a hotel in Paris as we can stand. (I have previously stayed a night in what must have been the worst hotel in Paris on a business trip with my last company; followed by a night at Le Grand Intercontinental, one of its best to make up for it.)

Then began the calls from the VC. First, he couldn't find an airline flight, and was asking if I could make his arrangements. I managed to parry this unusual request of a CEO's time to the VC's own executive assistant who seemed unaware of the trip at all. Once we got past the flights, finding a suitable hotel was the next issue. I dutifully passed on the coordinates of the hotel we would be in, and can only assume all is now well.

In the interim, we have somehow acquired a "French representative"—a VC Buddy of our lead investor, whom he recommended as a tactical expert on the ground. Since both my partner and I speak French, it is unclear why we need this gentleman, but the investor was clear that "no" is not an acceptable answer, and so we have another body to deal with. Since he is touted as someone familiar with Vivendi, we figure the rep could still be of value; he should have some valuable insight for us on Vivendi's internal chain-of-command, and identify the decision-makers we need to meet with and convince.

One concern—without having ever met or even spoken with 'Le Buddy'—is that he does not live in Paris, and in fact we will have to pay for him to travel up from the South of France and to stay in a hotel in Paris for the duration of our trip.

A second, bigger concern is that we are being forced (and I seriously mean forced) to pay him five thousand dollars for his week of work. I suggested to our VC that we "pay for what we get" meaning we would reimburse Le Buddy's trip and fees assuming he actually did us some good. Our investor is good at games like this though, and simply told us he'd bill us directly from his own expenses, to pay his friend. Having no real choice, I agreed to just have him bill us directly, so at least our financials would accurately reflect Le Buddy was under contract to us, not the investors, and perhaps allow us to exert some corporate control over him. Were he officially to be on the payroll of our venture capitalist, I doubt we would even see him, though we'd still be expected to pay his expenses.

We leave tomorrow for what will certainly be an interesting and eye-opening trip. I hope I will have nothing but positive entries on the events and people we encounter along the way. One omen does not bode well: Jay just told me that the French word for "buddy" is actually "copain". Given he'll be with our lead investor, co-pain is quite an appropriate label.

"Bon Chance," as our imminent hosts would say. "Bon Chance...et priez Dieu[1]"indeed.

---

1.   Trans: Good Luck...and Pray to God

March 29th: Paris in the Spring

This entry is a little delayed, but I had no time to write while I was away. It was an unforgettable trip to Paris; luckily not my first or I'd think a great deal less of France and the French than I do. My opinion of our lead investor on the other hand could hardly fall further than it managed to on this trip. Le Buddy, the French Rep was the perfect Robin to his 1960s camp version of the caped crusader: "Holy investment, Batman! You are the greatest venture capitalist, this side of the Seine!"

All the gory details I care or dare to remember follow here. The parts without Batman or Robin present are described as rapidly as they seemed to pass; if the rest of the description seems interminable, it's because our time with the VC and Le Buddy were far beyond that in reality.

We arrived in France the morning before our meeting, to find messages waiting from the rep. He was trying to find out where the VC was, as he was meant to pick him up from the airport and had no idea when he was arriving. We had no idea either, and half a day was spent figuring out where and when the great man was coming in. Eventually the time-delayed response to our calls to Chicago came through; we discovered he was expected to check into the five-star Sheraton near Place de la Concorde. As my partner and I surveyed our small, bare rooms, we wondered why we didn't think of checking into an opulent luxury-class hotel too.

After some more coordination mishaps, we finally arranged to meet for dinner at the Sheraton to discuss strategy for the next morning. Thus far, our French rep had been a dud—offering no information on Vivendi and never spending any time in Paris at all, but eking out an existence somewhere in the French countryside working on construction projects.

We walked the streets of Paris over to the Sheraton from our hotel—one of the pleasant benefits of our VC's hotel being situated in a beautiful part of the city. Though they are all beautiful parts I suppose. Arriving at the hotel, we called upstairs and ended up waiting for our investor in the hotel bar at his request; he was not quite ready to come down from his room for our working dinner.

We were quite surprised by what he brought with him when he did come down. A rather young and attractive woman was on his arm. Certainly not his wife: looking closer to his son's age—about ten years ago. She was introduced vaguely as an artstudentcomefashionmodel; we never did figure out exactly how they ended up together, but I can only hope no money-changed hands. Not so much from a moral standpoint, but that I'll be paying the bill when the VC sends his trip expenses.

Dinner was wonderful, but there was no discussion of work. Attempts to bring up the topic appeared to bore our artsy companion. She pouted, sighed, twirled her hair, and constantly tugged down the hem of her black cocktail dress as she squirmed around in her seat; our VC ravenously stared at her thighs with every shift of her skirt.

The French say "ennui" goes beyond simple boredom. I finally understand what they mean. Combining teenage angst, a haughty air of artistic superiority and a disdain for the unfashionable that might have been from being self-assuredly beautiful, a youthful fashionista, or just being French, she made it abundantly clear that this was simply the most boring time she could be having in Paris tonight. 'Boring' her was what our VC was evidently looking to do, but not in the same way.

We determined that we would meet again the following morning and discuss strategy for an hour before heading over to our meeting at the modern La Défense sector of offices on the edge of central Paris. Le Buddy—who we had just been informed was actually charging us five thousand dollars *per day* for the two days in Paris he was assisting us, thereby doubling his fee—said he would work out transportation logistics and make sure we had what we needed to make a good impression. My partner and I decided to head back early to prepare for the meeting and get over our jetlag so we would not seem unenthused when pitching the next day.

In the morning, we arrived back at the Sheraton to find our VC again not ready, and after a half-hour wait he made it down to the lobby along with the French rep. Where the rep was staying (we had thought he said he was sharing a room with the VC) and what he, our VC and the young lady might have been doing the previous night were unclear. Not something we particularly wanted to contemplate, but they did seem to have had an enjoyable time and a very late night. There was no sign of the young lady this morning, which Jay and I were grateful for.

As we headed out of the hotel, we asked Le Buddy where the transportation he had arranged was. "We'll just catch a cab" he replied cheerily, seemingly oblivious to the dirty looks Jay and I gave each other.

The Sheraton is a major business hotel, and at that time of morning, businesspeople were plentiful and cabs were not. After around twenty minutes of first waiting for a cab and then my partner and I racing up and down the street trying to hail one while Le Buddy and VC waited at the hotel entrance chatting, we finally were able to locate a cab and pile into it.

"Vivendi offices, La Défense" we said and the cab driver rolled off into the creeping Paris morning rush hour, as Jay and I began to feel the awful prickly sensation of perspiration building up after our exertions chasing our cab's brethren. There is nothing worse than going into a meeting hot and sweaty. With full suits, shirts and ties, carrying laptops and marketing materials, we had managed to take ourselves right to the edge of that feeling. With the windows rolled down (no A/C in the cab of course), we were cooling off, but now we were looking windswept and scruffy which were almost as bad.

Finally, we made it to La Défense, with a few minutes to spare but having had no real discussion on strategy for the meeting. It turns out the area is a huge complex of office parks, and the address that Le Buddy had given the cab driver did not exist. We drove around vainly searching for signs indicating Vivendi, or any other name that sounded familiar. Eventually we gave up on this tactic and asked to be dropped off in the center of the largest group of buildings and to take our chances asking for directions from workers who were scattered around the plaza we stopped at.

After another twenty minutes of being sent in multiple directions, we finally found someone who knew where we needed to go, and with that, we were in the Vivendi building—late, sweating, disheveled, but at least at the meeting.

We met with a mid-level manager in our technology area, and did an adequate job of explaining our products and how they could assist Vivendi. Enough to be invited back the following day for an additional meeting, this time with a key decision-maker.

With a little effort, we found ourselves a cab and headed back into Paris to enjoy an afternoon that Jay and I decided to spend sightseeing and relaxing. We knew we'd just be selling the same story the next day, so there was little to have to prepare for. It was great to be free of VC, Le Buddy and frankly of thinking about work at all. This was after all, Paris in the Spring! A good meal in the Latin Quarter after looking out on the old city from the Eiffel Tower at twilight relieved the stress of the morning and put us back into a positive frame of mind—that and a good long bitch session at how our VC always managed to recommend losers that somehow even made him look good. Okay, so we hadn't stop thinking about work completely, but the venting felt good.

The next morning, it was back to more of the same. We headed to meet our investor again. This time, he had another meeting to go to, so would not be accompanying us, and it turned out his meeting was in the building next to Vivendi. He was happy to have Le Buddy stay with us though, to assist in our efforts. Though we felt there was little benefit to this, we agreed rather than cause any friction at this point. Keeping our thoughts on Vivendi was paramount and making a great impression on the decision-maker was the point of this whole trip.

We were able to hail a cab more readily this morning, but in this case, the cab would not take four passengers, so Le Buddy hustled me, Jay and the VC into the cab and agreed to grab another cab and meet us at our destination. Our investor wanted to be dropped off at his meeting first; we were happy to be rid of him and had a quick discussion on how to avoid Le Buddy from talking too much in our own meeting.

Arriving at La Défense again (this time without any directional problems), we piled out and headed to the Vivendi offices, looking around to see where Le Buddy was. Given we had an extra stop, we assumed he would be waiting for us, but with no sign of him and a few minutes before the meeting time, we decided to head up to the thirtieth floor of their impressive, modern architecture building (though less impressive due to the numerous taller, more imposing buildings surrounding it) and set-up our presentation. We did not want to keep Vivendi waiting two days running.

The meeting began smoothly as we explained the basics of our company and our products; we were ready to talk about details of what projects Vivendi were seeking to initiate and how we could plug into them. We had been going for around twenty minutes of our allocated one-hour meeting.

A knock at the door announced the entrance of Le Buddy, who rushed in apologetically. We explained that we were in the middle of discussions and had covered all the introductory topics: "Take the hint, sit down and shut-up," our faces told him in no uncertain terms. He nodded his understanding and then proceeded to make the strangest speech I have ever seen in any language.

While my French was a little rusty, I was able to easily follow an extremely long-winded personal introduction of Le Buddy to the Vivendi manager, including: who he was; what his business was (something to do with sewage? My poor French no doubt gave me that impression); how he knew our investor; and that he was newly on-board to completely represent our company in any negotiations in France. Jay and I looked at each other, slightly confused by this last point. We were quickly more frustrated however, by Le Buddy launching into an introduction of our company and its products. Beyond the fact we had done this already, he was managing to get enough of the details wrong that our Vivendi contact was now beginning to look confused, both by these contradictions, and by the existence of Le Buddy at all.

I managed to hold up Le Buddy long enough to explain we were done with the introduction of the company, and he nodded as if I simply meant: "skip to the next part of your speech".

Proving our collective embarrassment and confusion were mere shadows of what was to come, Le Buddy began a speech directed at the Vivendi manager in praise of Vivendi's CEO—Jean Marie Messier—that I still can't get my head around enough to describe in all its glory; I paraphrase (and dramatically shorten) it here:

"Jean Marie Messier is a great man. Not just great, but a genius. You must be honored simply to work under him. His abilities are unsurpassed in the business world. He is more than the greatest businessman in France—he has taken over the world. Have you met him? I wish I could meet him, or even be in his presence. I am sure you felt inspired just to be in the same room, but to talk to him would almost have been too much. Too much for me, certainly. He has built Vivendi from a water company to a global power in all industries in five years. FIVE YEARS! He is the new Napoleon. I can't believe we are meeting you, and I have an opportunity through you to join his armies in taking over the world…"

I can't write anymore of the speech. It was too bewildering; and as scared as we were, our Vivendi counterpart looked worse: he seemed to be gauging whether leaping out of the thirtieth-floor window would be preferable to hearing any more. I would have taken my chances on the concrete below, but was more tempted to toss Le Buddy out of the window first to ensure a soft landing.

As we all squirmed uncomfortably, I tried to interrupt forcefully enough to stop the Messianic (or Messier-anic?) diatribe. My third attempt was successful, but the damage was already done. There really was no way to explain how we were not really associated with this crackpot in the time we had left. Polite information exchange proceeded for a few more minutes and our time was up. I promised to follow-up immediately, hoping that I might be able to stem the bleeding with Le Buddy out of the loop.

Jay and I stood in the elevator alternately fuming and cringing, as Le Buddy excitedly proclaimed how well the meeting seemed to have gone. I mentally restrained my hand from hitting the emergency-stop button and making our companion the late Le Buddy: "Le Buddy c'est Mort", his eulogy would begin.

We headed out of the building and down the street to meet our investor, who had been meeting with LVMH, the luxury-branded goods company. Louis-Vuitton, Moët and Hennessy are all recognizable brands across multiple markets, but are in fact all part of the same single, huge conglomerate. Why our investor would be meeting with them, or more accurately, why they would be meeting with him, remains a mystery. In any case, it seemed that his meeting had not gone as well as he'd hoped—at least he wasn't walking out of the building with any bottles of vintage champagne.

I wanted to get away from La Défense as quickly as possible; to get away from Le Buddy; to get away from our investor; to go hole up with Jay in some French café and drown my sorrow in café au lait and crêpes. It was too early for 'bière et vin' but those would come later. We were flying out the next day, and all I wanted to do was enjoy Paris on what would undoubtedly be our last business trip to the city related to Vivendi.

May 11th: Big Deal

We signed our first big revenue deal today. Or at least, we're about to sign it. First we need to actually be sure we can deliver a product. However, I've promised Al that we will deliver everything he promised the customer, and I've promised Jay that I'll kill him if he can't get it done. He told me I had sold out by turning my back on my technical background by committing to a salesman's promises without checking if the developers can actually do the work. I laughed as I told him it feels much better promising the world than having to build it in six days.

One problem with going after this deal is that it has moved the entire focus of the company off of building our main product that our long term future is based on, and onto completing a specialized product just to sell to this customer to make a quick buck. For now though, a quick buck is what we are sorely in need of. According to our investors, pointing to big name customers (and we are bringing together two with this product) and sustained revenues as they sell our bundled solution for months and years to come, will land us our next round of funding. The fact it will take several months of development followed by several months of lag-time to be paid, as the product moves through the sales channel, is not lost on us.

My biggest fear is that as we point to the future revenues, potential investors will sit on their hands waiting until we have a few months of revenue checks coming in, before committing to us. It's the standard VC way: if there's a reason to wait, you wait; if there's no reason to wait, you wait until there's a reason to wait.

Still, having a project with real income at the end of it helps focus our team, and everyone has a renewed excitement at the potential of seeing our first sold component and being able to point to what we hope is a well publicized and widely marketed product and say we're a key part of it.

I remember in my last company, we shipped millions of products and I could go to the local store and find a box on the shelf with our logo on it. Having my brand, my product out there where ordinary people could buy it was quite a feeling. I have that feeling again today, though we still have a lot of work to get us to that point.

This is just the beginning I hope of what will be many deals, many products on shelves, and many revenue checks. After our disappointment in Europe, we needed something to raise our spirits and this deal has been timely. I am finally doing something more than spending our venture capitalists' money: I'm bringing in some of my own.

I feel like I just moved out of my parents' basement and finally have my own spending money. A long way still from the mansion, sports car and a hot girl-friend (to carry on the analogy), but at least I can pay for my own corporate equivalent of pizza.

June 30th: Jobs to India—Part II

Disaster! That's the only word to describe it. Well, perhaps incompetents, liars, or scam-artists would work too. Okay, so 'scam-artists' is technically two words. Each of these terms describes our Indian contractors well though.

They are clearly incompetent, based on the joke of a beta software version they delivered us after months of work by supposedly a dozen engineers. What they produced can only be described as a week's work from a first year undergraduate programmer. In fact, I've seen middle-school computer geeks who have produced better software than what we just received.

The incompetence clearly runs contrary to the promises of expertise we were given back in January. My conclusion is that the contractors were lying when they sold us on their services; while Jay suggests we not jump to conclusions yet, I would say we have been scammed.

It's not easy to admit to ourselves that we've been had, and Jay walked out of the office this morning when I harshly (but I believed fairly at the time) put the onus on him to have figured that out well before today.

In retrospect (and based on discussions I had with the lead engineer at our end), the Indians have been very good at making it seem like things were on schedule. They provided weekly updates, and the only sniff of a problem was when they kept making excuses when we demanded code samples from them to see how they were designing things. Since we weren't sleuthing for major problems and simply wanting to see if there were stylistic differences between their development methods and our own, no one caught that blip on the radar; and we just got torpedoed as a result.

We have paid out a lot of money, for very little progress. A serious situation, and it's the first time I feel like I've failed in my role as CEO. The important thing now is how to rescue the situation. We've decided to confront the contractors and demand that they get us back on track ASAP. My brief call to their sales rep this afternoon summoning him to our offices tomorrow seems to make this a workable solution. I just wonder how much time we've really lost, and whether it's better to cut these guys loose now, rather than risk them screwing up and delaying us further: "Fool me once, shame on you; fool me twice…"

October 4th: The French Riviera

Jay—between coughs and sneezes—told me a tale of pillage and assault today. Unfortunately the former was attempted on our company and the latter on young French maidens...by our lead investor.

I had sent Jay to Cannes, France for a major tradeshow and conference at which we were showing our wares, in the booth of one of the biggest industry players who recently became a strategic partner. This was an opportunity to demonstrate our solution not just to the partner but also to all of their customers. If their customers liked us, we'd have a great chance to be bundled into their solution by default, which would generate huge revenue potential, and make selling our solution part of their marketing focus. Given they are one of the top five suppliers in the world, and this was considered one of the top couple of business events of the year, to say we were excited by the potential is an understatement.

The one downside was that we had to tell our investors all of this. We were eager to tell them about landing the partnership deal: one of only five companies worldwide chosen to partner our new friend, the industry leader. An unrivaled chance to be promoted by them as a preferred solution. This news impressed the VCs, but on hearing the event was taking place in France, our lead investor was positively orgasmic. He immediately volunteered to attend the show along with Jay, to help promote the company and assist with potential deal making.

Jay, Al and I all silently shook our heads: the only promotion would be self-promotion by the VC; the only deal making would be between him and whatever teenage girls he managed to troll for and impress using our expense account. Jay looked plaintively at me as we both recalled our trip to Paris. I shrugged and replied back into the phone that we'd be delighted to accept all the assistance our lead investor could provide, and suggested he should in fact work right in the booth on the show-floor alongside Jay. I narrowly avoided the pen that Jay fired at my head as I said this.

"Look at it this way," I said later, "at least you'll get breaks for lunch and coffee now...though I'm not sure I'd let our investor touch any of the equipment...or freak out our partners by hitting on any women in the booth...or talk to any customers—or anyone for that matter—since he still seems to have no idea what we do exactly."

Jay's problems began almost immediately on his arrival to Cannes. He managed to catch a nasty bout of the flu on the flight over, and was a dead man walking as he headed for the show. This was a three-day event, and the first day passed without incident, other than Jay hacking up a storm. He was very impressed both by our partner, and the other small companies they had chosen along with ours, to show off their value-add solutions to the big customers trawling for new and exciting technologies. The thing that struck Jay most was that each of these companies had their own investors at the show, and they were doing everything from bringing back coffees and lunches for hardworking booth staff, to working the booth themselves, to going out and hunting down decision-makers to bring back to show off their products to. Meanwhile, Jay had seen no sign of our lead investor, and had no idea if he was even in the country. I confirmed with his office that he was indeed in France, but beyond that I couldn't tell Jay what might be happening.

On day two, Jay was looking and feeling worse. Our booth partners apparently suggested Jay ought to leave the show floor, both in genuine concern for his health and likely some trepidation over catching the flu from him. As our only representative—other than our AWOL investor—Jay had no choice but to stick around and do his best to sell our product with a hundred-and-one degree fever.

Finally, near lunchtime, our VC showed up at the booth. He seemed angry and distracted. Apparently his cell-phone wouldn't work in France, and he had urgent calls he needed to make. Exactly to whom these calls would be, since Jay was the only one he ought to be concerned with speaking to, and precisely why he couldn't call using a landline phone to make them were unclear. He asked Jay to join him for lunch, even though this meant shutting down our demo at the booth with no one else to operate it. Feeling he had no choice, Jay headed out of the conference hall, to grab a bite to eat, though he wasn't sure he'd be able to keep any food in his stomach given his condition. On leaving the show floor, the lead investor was suddenly joined by a young, attractive woman. She was going to be joining Jay and the VC at lunch, and they were then heading off in the afternoon apparently, no doubt for the kind of fun and excitement that we would not want to even think about.

This young lady turned out to be an Air France flight attendant who the VC managed to pick up on his trip over from Paris to the nearby Nice airport. The lure of an all-expenses trip to Monte Carlo and Cannes had snared her, and our investor looked like an angler pleased with himself at landing another tasty fish.

If ever anyone needed proof that money and power trump smarm and creepiness, our lead investor is all the validation you'd need.

Jay made another mistake, in his fevered haze. He mentioned that his cell-phone did work in France. As lunch ended, the VC borrowed the phone "for a few minutes". Jay had to get back to the show floor, so he left the VC and giggling flight attendant—who looked like she was trying hard to keep herself off the lead's lap, and failing miserably—as the lead began dialing numbers and evading his frolicking playmate. "If I didn't feel so much like vomiting from the flu," Jay said, "I would have thrown up from watching them."

An hour later, the VC showed back up at the booth, to hand back Jay's phone; he was complaining that the battery had died, and he still had calls to make. This meant he had to take off to find another phone, but he'd try to be back later in the day, or offered to take Jay to dinner. Luckily, the show had a formal dinner for attendees that evening, and so Jay was booked. The investor sounded disappointed at not being able to spend his evening regaling Jay with tales of his sexual conquest, but it did free him up to hit the casinos in Monte Carlo, so on balance he appeared as happy as Jay was at avoiding him.

Day three, Jay said he was barely able to stand. He headed to the show, but this time was ordered by our show partners to go back to his hotel room to die in peace. The last day of a show is usually quiet; all the decision-makers catch early flights home, so everyone agreed it was for the best if Jay rested up. There was no sign of the lead investor, who apparently was still in the area, but clearly enjoying the Cannes marina or riding first class on Air France so to speak.

While the show was still a success, the difference between our investor's priorities and actions and those of the other startups surrounding us, served simply to reinforce something a venture advisor once told me. At the time, I considered his advice to be useless (and much of it was), but in retrospect, I think he was right on the ball: "You exist simply to give your VC entertainment value. The more you can entertain, the more funding you can get."

His opinion on why we weren't raising more funds was that we just weren't "fun" enough. I was still on a path of fiscal responsibility, building a solid business and creating value being the ways to raise funding from venture capitalists, so I dismissed his complaints.

As time has gone on, I have come to realize how sadly correct that venture advisor was. Our investor simply uses us as a vessel through which he can travel to exotic locales, speak with rich, powerful or beautiful people, and impress them by pointing to us as an example of his own power and success. As soon as we are unable to meet his ever-increasing wanderlust and celebrity lifestyle, we will have lost his confidence and enthusiasm.

Building a business that will bring him a return on his investment is secondary to him having—as the venture advisor suggested—"a good time on our dime in the meantime".

November 14th: Jobs to India—Part III

I had my first yelling match with a fellow CEO today. The head of our Indian contracting firm showed up at the offices for an impromptu meeting. He had traveled from India to the United States to drum up sales, and decided to meet us before heading for the airport to fly back.

I was sorely tempted to turn him away, saying we were too busy digging to see him. "Digging?" I'm sure he'd say quizzically. "Yes," I would bitingly reply, "digging ourselves out of this monumental hole you put us in with your lies and incompetence."

So I wasn't able to play out that little fantasy, but the reality was almost better. I believe Jay has a new belief in my ability to be a tough-talking CEO. Which is great, except for the fact that it doesn't exactly solve our problem of how we dig ourselves out of the hole.

My discussion with the Indian CEO began quietly enough. We ran through the history of our relationship, ending with the failed attempt by the contractors to get us "back on track" over the free-of-charge months of hard effort they promised us, but which we saw little evidence of, and which they were now trying to bill us for.

Things went downhill quickly. The CEO insisted that all our problems had been fixed to our satisfaction. I stared coldly at the local sales rep we normally dealt with, as I questioned where the CEO could have gotten that idea. The rep squirmed uncomfortably; he tried to cover himself, first angering me by overselling what we had said to him (which was actually that we were completely dissatisfied—he had decided to simply drop the "dis"); and then infuriating his own CEO by back-pedaling on what the contractors had actually accomplished. This was news to the CEO, who stared stiffly at the rep, presumably contemplating a murder on foreign soil for a few seconds, before regaining his composure.

I explained the situation as it now stood. We were not going to pay the Indians for any further work, based on their inability to meet requirements throughout our working relationship. The Indian CEO started to open his mouth in protest, but I silenced him with a raised hand as I explained we would also not be paying the last few invoices they sent us (bearing in mind we had already spent a large six-figure sum on past invoices when we were being assured work was proceeding apace in India, with the first major software delivery coming).

The CEO was livid. We owed well over a hundred thousand dollars in fees to him by his reckoning. I could see him mentally thinking about the five million rupees this translated to. A lot of money.

"That is completely unacceptable," he said. "We have worked those hours and you must pay us for them."

A reasonable argument to be sure. I countered with reason of my own: "Actually, you failed to provide us any satisfactory deliverables in a timely fashion, based on your own milestones. As a result, we have no evidence that your employees worked those hours at all. As soon as you deliver us what you promised, I will pay your invoices. Not a dollar or a minute before that though." I spoke firmly and confidently. I had decided in advance it was not going to matter what he said to me. The fact that we didn't have a hundred thousand in the bank to pay him anyway gave me a superior sense of bravado.

At this point, the Indian CEO exploded in a rant of indignant economics and bullying. "We are a public company, sir. We have to report our earnings to our stockholders and to analysts. We cannot have one of our customers refuse to pay us what they owe." His voice was rising with every sentence. "You may be a small company, but we are a large corporation with hundreds of employees, and we expect to be paid." He was yelling now, and had switched from wildly flailing his arms around to thumping his fists on the conference table: "THIS IS VERY UNPROFESSIONAL. ABSOLUTELY UNPROFESSIONAL. YOU WILL KINDLY (thump) PAY US (thump) WHAT (thump) YOU OWE (thump)...NOW (bang)."

Jay and the Indian rep looked horrified. I might have been more moved—certainly more amused—had he whipped off a shoe and 'Kruscheved' us instead.

I had planned to be reasonable, but I know bullies are best confronted: "I really don't care about your stockholders or your analysts. I *am* sure that they will be very interested in your misrepresentation of your business and expertise, and your inability to deliver on your contracts in a timely fashion. I'm *very* sure your customers would want to hear about that too."

The Indian CEO's bluster seemed to be fading. Before he could respond, I moved in for the kill: "Now, thanks to your company's incompetence, I have to go find another contracting firm to get us back on track. And I'm going to be using the money we owe you to pay them to do it. If I were you, I'd walk out of here happy we're not coming after the rest of the money we already paid you. You don't want to piss me off any more than you already have. The best you're going to get here is walking away with the money you already ripped off of us. Keep after us and I will make sure you have a lot more to worry about than explaining away an unpaid invoice in your quarterly earnings statement."

There was a strange gurgle from the CEO, as if words were trying to form, but his mouth was no longer up to the task. I continued to stare him down, leaving him in no doubt as to the seriousness of what I was saying.

That was it. He stood up, and walked out of the room, his pet rat, the sales rep, scuttering across the room behind him, nervously glancing back as if I was going to pounce on him there and then.

Jay looked at me as I shrugged with a: "I guess we'll see what happens next" look on my face. I think our point was made and they will see reason given the very solid ground we're on. We'll be sure to circle the wagons though, just in case the attacking Indians decide to come back.

February 11th: A Motley Crew

Every company has its share of characters; employees with big personalities or egos, quirks or idiosyncrasies, that are unique to each individual, and yet familiar no matter where you work.

It is the diversity of backgrounds that make working together interesting, and I am pleased by the fact we have so many employees that bring their own unique perspective on everything from working style to the kind of cuisine we eat together every Friday. We have Lebanese and Israelis working side by side with Cubans, Indians, Scots and Chinese. We're not quite at fifty-fifty on our male-female ratio, but I'm committed to pushing for more qualified women, if only because our female developers are quietly productive, while we have many prima donnas in our senior, male engineering core.

One thing I am most proud of is our company sponsoring a scholarship through the Society of Women Engineers (SWE) for high school girls to pursue an engineering or technical degree at the university-level. I was especially pleased to award this year's scholarship to a young woman, about to undertake an electrical engineering degree, who I also (by sheer coincidence) happened to be mentoring in another terrific organization, called MentorNet.

The chance to influence the next generation of women I could be hiring a few years from now is one of the most rewarding aspects of having a corporation through which I can make a difference.

In addition to this corporate scholarship, we're trying to reward our employees for any community work they do, as well as promote their own education and betterment. I really want our company to be more than just a place to pick up a paycheck, it should be an enabler for growth or benefit should an employee seek it. After all, I started out as a computer geek, and ended up a CEO and business executive, having passed through a long time spent marketing and branding too. Quite a journey, and possible only through many mentors, managers and corporate enablers that I have been fortunate enough to encounter.

At the same time as offering these benefits, I am frustrated by some employees' expectations and their demands for preferential treatment, or an attitude that they are indispensable and can therefore push their boundaries and their luck.

I recognized a "them and us" attitude from management in the past, but it is interesting now that I am in management, that there are employees who seek to drive this wedge also. The old phrase about "a good day's work for a good day's pay" may need dusting off, given the view of certain employees that they are doing me a favor showing up to do their jobs. While such employees are few and far between, it is their ability to stir up grumblings from the rest of the pack that can be most detrimental. I have discovered that employees are generally content, unless they believe someone else is more content than them.

For the most part though, managing almost thirty people at this point has been a wonderful experience. There is always a new nugget to discover about each individual, their aspirations or doubts as we move along. Being around this group is the best part of the job without a doubt. Even when I am having to deal with an engineer complaining about the wording of our drug-policies in the employee handbook, and wondering exactly why he's so worried about the policy, and why he knows so much about the differing categories of restricted prescription drugs. Or the needs of an engineer for a special, thousand-dollar office chair, or of another's requirements for adjusting the air-conditioning five times a day.

I find that as we grow, I have less chance to interact with the employees, and even our Friday lunches are being seen as an annoying disruption by many employees, rather than a chance to get together and just hang-out. In a way, I miss our original startup family, when we were just a little baby company. It seems we've grown into a troublesome toddler...I dread to think what our teen-age years will be like!

June 3rd: New Realities

Due to the collapse of the markets and dramatic devaluation of companies that has accompanied it, we have been forced to re-price our private stock. This involves converting the bridge funding our investors have provided after their original Series-A investment into additional shares at a reduced price. In effect this makes our shares worth about one quarter of their prior value. Not good. It also increases dramatically, the ownership share to our investors. Definitely not good. Still, while this kind of dilution is never a happy occasion for an entrepreneur, we are pragmatic in understanding it allows us to continue to operate and to seek out new revenues and funding under new market realities.

The bridge funding we have received is in the form of convertible notes: providing loaned money that we pay back in the form of additional stock in the company. These loans do not come cheap. They pay out significant interest rates—the kind that would make your credit card company shudder (or smile enviously).

The advantage of course is this is cash (valuable and tangible) for stock (intangible). It is the interest accruing on these funds that ha become a bane on my existence.

We have been trying to close our re-pricing quickly: to halt the growing stock-interest and present a cleaner corporate structure for potential investors. This process began in January with our investors' infamous lawyer Dick. It hopefully ends now with new counsel on the investors' side, but with some already missed payrolls on ours.

On Wednesday, the last few documents were complete. We picked Thursday as a closing date and awaited review and approval from the investors. One of the key issues was the exact amount of interest accrued, based on this closing date, and the number of shares this translates to. The investors missed Thursday as the closing date, because their accountant, Iris, didn't review the documents in time. This meant I had to regenerate a number of dated documents, including a recalculation of the interest for the extra day. I dutifully sent this package to Iris once again on what was now Thursday. She did not review it until Friday, pointing out the interest calculation (now a day old again) was incorrect. I clarified the reasons and told her to go ahead and just update the single interest figure and we would be done. "No," she said. "You need to update all the docs and re-send them to me." I silently packaged everything again to send, all the while, raging internally (both within myself and within the company) that the investors are pulling this stunt again. I will skip Friday's events as they read pretty much the same; only we now hit the weekend, so I had the added fun of adding three extra days this time, since VCs—as we now know—don't fund on Fridays. Today—Monday—almost a week since we were actually done—Iris read her email, reviewed the numbers one last time, and finally blessed the funding; and in the drawing out of the process cost us more shares and another delayed payroll.

The cynic in me continues to question whether a process that benefits the investor by being dragged out interminably leads them to find reasons to delay. We have plenty of examples of this in our history with our VCs to consider this likely.

It is widely accepted that VCs know that time is typically against the entrepreneur looking to get funds in the bank to keep moving forward—often with payrolls or invoices in critical condition, needing a cash-injection imminently. Time pressures mean they can squeeze a slightly better deal as a result. In Iris's case, I wonder if it is less calculated and more simply an inflexible employee who could conclude there is a more efficient and productive way to do business, but chooses not to follow it.

The realization that simple transactions with our lead investor are always problematic and complex interactions almost impossible was the first thing we recognized as troubling back when we first closed funding. The second lesson learned has been far more significant. Our investors will not—or cannot—see that an extra hundred shares or extra five days to close funds is nothing compared to the damage done to the company. *Their* company. After all they are majority shareholders.

Missing a payroll is catastrophic to a company, as fears and concerns enter parts of employees' brains previously dedicated to doing their jobs. We have tried desperately to avoid these disruptions; unfortunately, we have been unsuccessful more often than we would hope. And when productivity drops, as employees spend time looking for other employment, updating their résumes, or just simply being distracted and disengaged, the loss is far more tangible than the gain in interest or shares to the investors in the business. When you are trying to hold a company together, it's hard to do anything beyond just asking employees for patience and loyalty. When you're not paying the employee and have no guarantees that you ever will be able to again, demanding productivity—demanding anything actually—is difficult at best, and disingenuous at worst.

While I am not able to tell our employees everything that has been happening in our funding processes, I have elected to honor my vow to keep them as informed as possible; I would recommend any entrepreneur err on the side of a realistic or pessimistic worldview in doing so, because invariably an optimistic view ends up seeming naïve when things go wrong. It seems better to pull off an unlikely but achievable success, than heroic defeat from a previously hyped victory.

I have found that my employees in general appreciate the honesty and are able to make an informed decision to stick things out with us (as they continue to do). In closing this re-pricing, we have given ourselves ninety more days—rather than the weekly living we've been slaves to for the last six months.

What is exciting is that we now have a promise of a further two million dollar investment via our lead VC, after the ninety days. My singular goal for the next three months is to close that funding and return our employees' faith, and eventually our investors' money too.

July 1st: Save Us Money? No Way

I am always confused by venture capitalists' relationship with money. While they are nitpicking over every penny in budgets or entrepreneurial compensation, they are just fine with spending on extravagances like expensive meals and meetings and retreats with their portfolio companies.

I am scheduled to head to New York City in two weeks for our secondary investor's own Annual General Meeting. I'm meant to present our company status, in a three-slide presentation. This means I'm likely to be spending about ten minutes doing something useful. The meeting is on a Tuesday, which of course is all the better, because I have to miss more weekdays traveling, and the cost is dramatically higher for flights without a Saturday night stay.

As I have friends in New York, I thought I might visit with them while I was on the "right" coast as they always call it (the implication being that the west coast is the "wrong" coast as opposed to the "left" one). By flying in on a Friday night and staying the weekend, I'd be able to stick around for Monday and return Tuesday after the investor meeting broke up. The alternative was to fly in on the Monday and leave the Tuesday, which is painful for a coast-to-coast trip.

Calculating the cost of flights, there was a seven hundred-dollar saving were I to include the Saturday night stay. While I had anticipated staying with friends in the city, I thought I'd see if the investors (who were picking up the tab for the trip) would be amenable to letting me stay two extra nights in the hotel they had recommended. This would cost an extra three hundred dollars total, but still save them over four hundred overall.

The investors of course didn't see things that way. They would rather I charged them more money to stick to their criteria. I was all set to do that, when I discovered they weren't actually going to make the arrangements anyway. I was going to have to do it, and then file an expense report to be reimbursed by them.

So I've decided to take the trip the way I want and submit my total expenses and we'll let the chips fall where they may. At this point, I'm tired of saving money for people who have no interest in being fiscally responsible themselves.

Why is the meeting in New York City? The investor is based in Washington DC, which means their entire organization is having to travel up to Manhattan and be put up in hotel rooms for a couple of days; all but one of the portfolio companies is each having to do the same for our ten minutes of useful activity. We have flights, hotels, cabs, and meals to be expensed. Why New York City? So a venture firm can get out of the office for a couple of all-expense paid days in Manhattan, with their flights, hotels, cabs and meals paid for.

Given that, why on earth would they care if I could save them money?

July 16th: VC Board Meeting in NYC

I'm not sure whether to feel happy or depressed. The stories I heard from many fellow portfolio companies at our VC's Board Meeting made our own attempts to survive seem positively triumphant.

I had my five minutes of stardom, surrounded by six hours listening almost exclusively to tales of woe from entrepreneurs who sounded like I have on the many occasions I've thought we were finally gone forever.

It is sad that I met so many of these same folks early on in our startup life and theirs too in most cases; we were full of enthusiasm and energy. I see some of the same faces, though a few seem to have been replaced already. Their expressions are not enthused or energetic. They are done. Defeated. One of the veteran CEOs I had met and befriended the last time we all got together pulled me aside to ask why the hell we were here at all. I had just returned from a side meeting we were all forced to have with a 'venture catalyst' company—supposedly able to provide advice and services to assist venture-backed companies in need of help. I had to concede it was a complete waste of our time, and the investor's money. The venture catalysts had asked me such generic questions that it was clear they had no understanding of our problems, or any likelihood of solving them for us. I expect to see the venture catalysts having the same devastated look of imminent collapse on their own faces by the end of the year based on their uselessness. Why the investors would not simply apply the money they paid to the catalysts directly to funding the portfolio companies was not immediately clear to any of us.

Everyone had a horror story to tell, and they (almost) made me feel that things weren't so bad for us after all. My veteran colleague told me he had laid off a quarter of his employees the day before he was forced to come out to this meeting. He was spitting bullets about having to leave his office under the circumstances. He privately admitted that he was going to have to cut another ten percent the day he got back. The story hit me particularly hard because the younger entrepreneurs, including me, had always looked upon this CEO as 'most likely to succeed' based on his experience and the fact his company was far more established and further along that the rest of us early-stagers. I could see the anger and frustration in his eyes as he said of the VCs: "they just don't get it."

The worst moment was when one pair of entrepreneurs was called upon to give their three-minute update. It turns out they have already run out of money and effectively shutdown just a few days ago. Their presentation was essentially a plea for a miracle cash injection from the investors present, laced with a bitter undertone that they were being forced to beg for their corporate lives in front of the rest of the pack who were howling and whining for funds just as loudly too.

I wondered what the investor's board members would say in response to all this doom and gloom. At least announce they had some more money for the last unfortunates, to give them a reason for having shown up: "your lives are spared...now pledge your undying loyalty to us and go forth and do our bidding". No such luck.

There's only one thing worse than traveling all this way just to speak for three minutes and that's to have traveled here to sing "thanks for the memories" to an unappreciative audience. I think I better start learning the lyrics; judging from the portfolio companies around me, it's going to be a choral performance next time we see each other.

End of Part Two

PART THREE: Down

August 15th: To Live or Die in LA

Time for another monthly board meeting. Actually, the time for the board meeting was two months ago, but the investors have been unable to meet with us, even though we've desperately needed to convene to make the tough decisions required to improve our currently impoverished condition.

We finally managed to get the VCs to California, but the closest they were going to be was in Los Angeles on other business, so we flew down to meet them at an airport hotel by LAX this morning. A wonderful use of our time and funds, but better than going another month or more without getting them on record as making the hard choices needed to keep ourselves operational.

Our fundamental problem (as always) is our rapidly diminishing bank balance, and—even with some decent revenue checks we're imminently expecting—the lack of long term stability needed to operate in an environment where closing a deal can take many months. It is very difficult to even commit to partnering at a trade show with industry leaders (as we have been) when we're not entirely certain we'll be around to meet the commitment. We do, of course, understand it's in the nature of business that you have to hope for the best even as you're planning for the worst. If you aren't able to do the planning though, you rapidly lose much of the hope.

We did accomplish two main action items, which is all I could have expected to get out of an hour in a hotel lobby.

First, we got continued buy-in to pursue the partnership we have been working on for months now, with the number one company in our industry. We believe this should lead to a deal for a major product launch early next year, which should in turn lead to a factorial increase in revenues in six to nine months. It should offer leverage with potential investors, whom we continue to hit as hard as we can, though with limited success due to the very long lead-times every startup is encountering in closing investments in the current funding environment.

Second, we reached agreement with the investors on receiving three months of funding in a single contribution at the end of this month, which will give us some of the stability we've been seeking. It has been a particular distraction to me that I have spent much of each four-week funded period making sure we would get the next month's money. While we appreciate the continued funding, it makes little sense for us or the investors to drip-drip the money to us, never quenching our thirst or giving us the energy to do anything but hold our parched mouths under the leaking faucet. The fact that this money was agreed to and arranged as a twelve-month bridge funding several quarters ago is what has caused me such annoyance. I understand the need for the company to demonstrate itself to be a smart investment, but that's the process we painfully confirmed months ago with all parties agreeing we would be viable through the rest of the year. To then spend all my time reassuring the investors of this fact on a daily basis has not been healthy for any of us.

Funding to take us to the end of the year without me having to spend every day begging for it is a huge step forward for us. I can get back to raising new funds, we can go after deals we know we'll be around to keep working on, and we can continue development on our partner project with that industry number-one that is likely our shortest and best path out of our current predicament.

Beyond this short-term shoring up of funds, we still have the two million dollar investment our lead VC mentioned to me previously as a future milestone. Strangely, we had precious little opportunity to discuss it today, though the lead did pull me aside to confirm he is working his side of the deal with his own investors. Once he has laid the groundwork, I am to jump in to wrap things up with all the necessary company specifics. Knowing we have some breathing room allows me to prepare whatever I need to now, to make sure we are ready when we imminently get a go-signal.

While it truly was an unnecessary waste of time and money to have to fly to LA today, it did buy us what we need most…time and money.

August 24th: Replace Me, but not with this Loser

Our investors have decided it's time for a change. What the change should be isn't entirely clear to any of us, but they want us to interview candidates to take a senior executive position at the company. Actually, it seems they only want us to interview one candidate: of their choosing. When I asked what position we're hiring for, the investors were vague. Deliberately vague. This would tend to suggest he's replacing me.

For a long time now, I've been suggesting we might want to look at bringing in a more experienced CEO: someone with a background either as an executive at one of the big industry players (so he can land more deals for us), or with strong ties to the financial industry (so he can land more funding for us).

As I have come across résumés (and with the downturn, I get bombarded with: "experienced startup executive" CVs daily), I have passed them on to the investors, asking them to review and approve bringing folks in to see if they might be suitable. They have never given the slightest hint of even looking at the résumés, never mind seriously considering the candidates.

I used to ask our secondary investor (the smart one), if there was something I should have been doing that I was not, simply because I didn't know any better. He would say that it was simply the horrendous venture market conditions that meant we were not able to get the kind of funding traction we needed. If I asked about bringing in a new CEO (allowing me to concentrate more on my other role as Chief Technology Officer), he would say he didn't see how anyone else could do much more than I was already doing, and it would just be another employee to feed from our very limited payroll.

So, despite all my offers of relinquishing the CEO position, the investors steadfastly ignored change at the top. Until now.

We recently had the great misfortune to lose our secondary investor (the person, not the fund) as a Board member. He was replaced with the head of our secondary venture firm, for reasons unknown, but likely related to his fervent support of us and our idea, and perhaps an inability to suffer our lead investor any further.

Our new Board member—the head of the venture firm—is eminently qualified and a very smart woman too. Except she has no idea what we do. She is also clearly too busy running the fund to put in the time to understand our product, industry or funding situation. Instead, she has abdicated all decision-making to our lead investor, accepting his world-view and suggestions at face value. I can't blame her really: coming to the situation as she has, she was always more likely to side with a fellow VC than an entrepreneur. I guess venture camaraderie and propriety stopped our previous (smart) secondary investor from explaining to his boss exactly how incompetent, incorrigible and insane our lead investor is.

In practice, this now means we live at the whim of our lead VC, who himself is running out of funds for his firm. It is a bad sign when your venture capitalist is going to be out of money before you are. As he has become more desperate with each passing month, he has been showing greater signs of instability, suggesting one crazy scheme after another, many conflicting with the others. I've been worried about what this all means, since he gets angry and frustrated if we don't do what he says, but I can't be trying to sell the company (one suggestion) while looking to buy out a public shell company (another) at the same time. Actually, I was able to do both of those things concurrently, but neither is accomplishable in the time we have left, try as we might, and relying on the lead's buddies to execute both. Increasingly, the directives involve bringing in VC Buddies on ridiculous contracts and stipends to assist us. Beyond assisting us in spending money on them, it is unclear what benefit they are providing.

Given the increasingly erratic investor behavior (well-intentioned perhaps, but horribly flawed in reality) I was actually relieved to hear that we had a potential addition or replacement finally coming in from Oregon. The VCs had passed up so many great résumés that we were excited to meet the single, mysterious candidate they considered worthy.

'Underwhelmed' would be, well, an underwhelming word to describe how disappointed we were with the man we met. I should have known there was something wrong when I had repeatedly asked for his résumé in advance, and none was forthcoming. All the investors would say is he was an expert in our industry and had run big operations in the past. What we actually had in front of us was a calculator-salesman. Fancy calculators, for a big-name company, but the bottom-line is, his major experience is in selling calculators. Not exactly our industry. Not someone with connections to the key players in our industry (to bring in sales) or to the venture industry (to bring in funding).

Jay, Al and I sat around after the candidate left to discuss exactly how clueless our investors must be if they saw this guy as a good fit. We always considered our lead investor to be dense. Our secondary investors had always managed to keep things on an even keel though, helping us navigate through troubled funding or business waters. With the switch of representative of the fund though, and the sobering effect of seeing their other portfolio companies in New York, for the first time, we're all feeling like the ship is heading straight for a huge iceberg and we have little margin for error to avoid it anymore. Interviewing the Captain of the Titanic today only made us feel more like we are doomed to a watery grave.

I'm not sure what is more depressing: the thought that we might not survive, or how bad the investors must think I am to have sent 'CalcuMan' to take over. Something just doesn't add up: I don't mind being replaced, but please, not with this loser.

September 1st: Furlough

Things are falling apart around us. We just missed another payroll today. Our LA meeting was meant to have led to having more funds in the bank by today, but yet again the day comes, the money does not. I called a meeting to explain the situation to the employees, and they are asking if they should ever expect another paycheck. I honestly couldn't give them an answer other than that it's very possible they may not.

As a result, I decided to put everyone on furlough. It seems unreasonable to have them in working, without being paid, and without me having any guarantee of ever paying them. So I told them all to go home, and as soon as we had some money, we would call them back in.

The employees are looking at me like I know I won't be calling them back in, and they should take the hint. It doesn't help that feeling that I told them all to feel free to come in to the office to use our resources if they want to look for other jobs, or do anything else that might help them prepare for unemployment. Jay also let them know they could file for unemployment and we'd sign off on any documentation. If we do get funds, they can take themselves back off the dole.

While I wasn't trying to suggest we're dead by hinting at it (I would have come out and just said it), I can't say we're not dead either. I did the only thing I could do, which is to say we are definitely dying, and unless the funding vaccine arrives in the next few days, the prognosis is not good.

September 10th: Sleepless

It's very late on Monday night and I can't sleep. Actually, it's 3am Tuesday morning at this point, so it's really September 11th. I haven't been sleeping well the whole week, but this is different, because tomorrow is going to be the worst day of my professional life.

We had one last conference call with the investors to close the funds they promised us back in August. The money is coming, but at a high price. Not that it's a price they are enforcing; we are in on the decision, which makes it all the worse.

We have to layoff two thirds of our employees. As soon as possible, which means tomorrow. I spent my evening figuring out with Jay and Al who we'll be keeping. Who we need and who is expendable. Except no one is expendable. If they were, they wouldn't be here.

Our new reality is that we need to keep our revenue deals supported, and await the continued promise of two million dollars from our lead investor. This money is meant to be in our account in October, and yet we're nowhere near any kind of paperwork that would make that happen, though he continues to assure me that by the end of next month, the money will be in our hands, and we can bring back many of the folks we're laying off tomorrow. Until then, we need to stop the financial bleeding and last two more months on a dramatically reduced burn-rate.

So I get to tell two thirds of our employees that they are history, though maybe only for a couple of months, and have them spend the time back in the parallel universe we all started in a lifetime ago when they were waiting for us to land our first funding, while looking for other jobs just in case we didn't.

Somehow I didn't see myself being back in this position again, but there is little I can do to change it, and it makes it no less painful to have to cut a staff that has been like a family over the last couple of years.

Maybe this is why corporate executives maintain a cold aloofness—that "them and us" attitude—that makes it easier to eliminate "them" when you need to. It also makes more sense to me now that losing some of the employees is preferable to losing all of them; if that is the choice you have to make. I still frown on companies doing so to simply increase record profits, but I wouldn't want our investors to hear that, or I'd likely be out of my CEO position faster than might already be the case.

Knowing I have no choice is not easing my conscience and it's not reducing my stress levels; it is not making sleep come any easier either. Keeping my emotions in check is much harder than I thought it would be, and I am worried that the effect this is all having in private as I lie here sleeplessly is going to be nothing compared to have to look everyone in the eye and tell them I'm letting them go.

What could be worse than being face-to-face with someone, informing them they no longer have a job, a paycheck, a livelihood?

September 11th: Terror

I'm not sure what to say about today. The whole world seems to have changed. The country was attacked. I have friends in New York and Washington. Thankfully I heard from all of them or about all of them, and they are safe. No, they are alive. Safe is something completely different, and right now, we don't know the meaning anymore.

Now for the worst part: as I sat glued to my television set from the earliest moments of the attacks (a side-effect of my sleepless night), I was thinking about what we had planned to do today at the office. Instead, I decided to close the office and let people stay home and understand what happened around the country today. I don't know if we do understand, or if we ever will exactly, but I did know I had no interest in dealing with the office or the business today, but in spending time with close friends and in contact with separated family.

Everyone I reached seemed more shocked than I was. I went out for a walk in the neighborhood and everyone I saw had emotion radiating out towards the rest of us. Many emotions, but all-powerful, like Hindu Gods each incarnating a facet of the human condition. In this case though, confusion, disbelief, anger, fear, sadness, love, hate…all manifested by those seeking understanding, community or vengeance—be it divine or human.

As someone whose skin-color matches the suspected-terrorists, but has nothing else in common with them, it was disconcerting to see the looks of fear or anger on the people around me, simply as I walked to the local coffee-shop. It's not like I could carry a sign saying: "I'm not Arab" or "I'm not Muslim" and in that fleeting thought, I recognized my own momentary prejudice in thinking being Arab or Muslim meant you supported the horrific acts any more than any other reasonable human being. Just because the terrorists might identify themselves as Arab or Muslim, does not mean Arabs or Muslims identify with them.

As a courtesy, I called our investors to tell them we had closed our offices and would not be putting our cutbacks into effect. I could not reach them and assumed they had closed too. Our DC investors in particular I am sure would be on lockdown, and I can only imagine the difference it makes to be living in the area targeted today.

Unfortunately, while I have no interest in my company compared to the world around me right now, this was also the day I was meant to shut much of it down. What happened today does not change our corporate circumstance, and makes it all the more likely we will be out of business completely. With the financial markets rocked so heavily; and in such a time of uncertainty about the future of everything, never mind venture capital or sales, revenues, or other things that seemed to vital to existence just yesterday, I think our two million dollars is gone as fundamentally as the country's sense of security.

I feel awful just thinking about anything just related to work on a day like this. It seems so inappropriate; so trivial. It's just that the trivial and inappropriate will be there tomorrow and the next day and the next and are not going away; 'life goes on' as they say, despite the collective need for us all to put life aside for awhile and just contemplate being alive.

September 12th: Misery

Everyone returned to work in zombified form today. We were going through the motions, mostly sitting in our offices checking the latest news via the web, or informally gathering to talk about what happened in little clumps that would form. As a busy office, we'd usually ignore each other as we walked by an open office door, on our way to the fax machine or fridge for a soda. You don't even say hello when you're passing the same person ten times a day, you just go about your business. Today, everyone took the time to stop. To ask about family, friends, anyone you might have known, or who was affected.

Amongst the stories, a miracle from one of my friends in New York. He had a good friend who worked high in the North Tower of the Trade Center. He assumed the guy didn't make it. He would have been in his office, above the crash-zone, so there's no way he could have survived. Even though I didn't know him, my friend's somber report reinforced my feeling that it didn't matter if you didn't know the victims personally, everyone will be affected by this for a long time to come, probably forever. Everything has changed. A couple of hours after hearing the initial report from my friend, he called me to say his friend was alive. It turns out he had gone out partying the night before, and woke up with a terrible hangover and late for work. He had been on the subway rushing to the office when the attacks occurred. "Just one of those random, lucky bastards I guess," is how he described himself through bitter tears to my friend. Everyone else at his office—as far as he knows—didn't make it.

There must be hundreds of stories like this that we will hear in the days to come. They provide optimism, and yet are sobering because for every lucky bastard there are others who were not.

As I sat in our meeting room with the whole company assembled around me, I finished discussing yesterday's events by saying that it perhaps reminds us of the things beyond work that matter in life. Not a great segue into the layoffs I was about to announce, but there was never going to be an easy way to relay that news.

The employees—to their immense credit—took the news in stride. I think they all understand exactly how hard it was for me to do what I'm doing, and how hard I've tried to prevent it. For those who are staying, they wanted to know if this was really just a way of giving them two-month's notice on their own termination, and all I could do was confirm it is quite probable. I think in a sense this made today's 'terminees' feel a little better about this not being personal, and just a practical decision based on who we needed around to make sure we at least got a little more revenue into the company, in the hopes that would help secure the two million dollars we're still banking on—no pun intended.

For the laid-off employees, I gave them the option of being terminated today (with all the paperwork that entails), or staying on furlough for a little while until we see if its likely we can bring them back. The advantages of the latter would be to maintain their health benefits a little longer and also retain their stock options; in the now highly unlikely event that we someday are worth a lot of money and their options can make them rich, they will retain their vesting schedule and granted stock. The investors had not given me an option to keep employees on furlough as opposed to cutting them loose today, but I really could care less what they want. I'm doing this because I have to, but only because I need their money. Without the money—and we're without the money today—I have no loyalty to them, and plenty to spare for my employees. Giving them some extra healthcare benefit time is the least we can do for them sticking it out, and the cost of coverage is a small price to pay. I'll cut costs or my own salary even further than I have already, to make sure we can do this.

I feel pretty devastated now that I look back on the day. I had to keep a professional, "CEO" demeanor as I announced our current plans; but here, alone, in the quiet of my own house, I don't have to keep up the pretense. I am tired, stressed and drained of all my energy. This has been the worst week of my life, and my hope and faith in things coming out positively have all but dissipated. For the first time, I feel like we're not going to make it. No matter how bad things were in the past, my gut-check always said we'd get through it; perhaps it's what happened yesterday on the east coast and the endless replays of the attacks and falling buildings that have me and the rest of the country in a deep pessimism and loss of faith.

I suddenly see darkness all around me, and it's not just because I'm sitting here with the lights off.

September 19th: Aftermath

We finally have money in the bank. Enough to last us two months, which should carry us through to the two million dollar cash injection in late October.

I'm back to feeling hopeful about our chances. Even with our shrunken team—back to a half dozen employees total—we have two major goals that will keep us busy, and if we can pull them off, we will be in great shape to re-launch ourselves, bring back the rest of the staff, and be on a path to generating big revenues. We have our existing revenue deals, and half the team is going to support them; the other half will be chasing the biggest customer in the world for our products. We already have the invitation to partner with them; we just need to deliver a working prototype to demo in their booth at this year's Fall COMDEX Show in Las Vegas. They are talking about millions of units next year shipping with our solution on board; that means big revenues and major exposure, provided we can make it to next year to collect. The two million dollars will allow us to easily achieve that, and from there, we'll be back on track to grow the company again.

This deal has been almost eighteen months in the making. The economic downturn had really hurt even the biggest players, and they are all moving incredibly slowly. I've heard of deals taking three years in some cases, so we're doing well to do it in half that. While it's taken us away from our core business and development goals for our products, we decided it was the best way to get us back to a fully-funded and revenue-positive state. The investors bought in, and we've put all our resources on landing these guys, beyond just protecting the deals we already have. With only three engineers left to work on the project, it feels like we're back to the days of our first COMDEX show, when we were pulling all-nighters to be ready for our launch; this re-launch is far more important, and it will bring us far greater rewards in terms of exposure and hard revenues, perhaps enough to not even need more venture capital. Given our experiences with venture capitalists, that can only be a good thing. Still, I need the ones we have to get us to the point that we not only close this deal, but also start receiving the revenue checks for shipping product. It's a painful delay that hurts every startup: you've done all the work, but you don't get paid for three to six months. Being around to pick up the check is all that matters now, and what a check it will be: we've heard predictions of anywhere from five to twenty million units sold in the first year, which translates to a number with a lot of zeroes after it for us. Beyond that, every other customer will want what the top dog does, and—having done the hard work for this customer—we'll be able to deliver it to everyone else with minimal tweaking. Always great to get paid over again for work you've already done.

So we know what we need to do: the engineers need to support two big projects with minimal resources for the next couple of months, and I need to make sure we're around to reap the rewards for all their hard work by making sure the investors keep their word. At this point, with the promise of big revenue checks rolling in six months from now, they'd be crazy to back out. Which is why I'm worried, of course.

October 1st: Budgeting for $2Mn

The start of another month, and of another payroll period. We have enough money for one of the former and two of the latter, and there's no sign of the two million dollars, even though I've been working with our lead investor on it every day.

I have however, started working out how to spend the money, even if it's not forthcoming. We needed to provide a budget document to the lead's investors who are providing him the two million to put into us. After working out how to make a few thousand dollars stretch for a month, pulling out our old growth plans and budgets is a lot of fun.

The one thing that makes this all seem more real is that I actually have exchanged information with the investor's investor, so I at least know he exists and knows who we are. The one conversation I had was very productive, and follow-up emails with him and our lead investor suggest things are moving forward. Not fast enough necessarily to be done by the end of this month, but hopefully at some point just after that, which is something we can live with—barely.

I'm not sure how much of this to tell employees—current and former—before I'm really sure it's going to happen. I've been burned, and burned them, far too often over every funding deadline in the past, to risk giving anyone false hope. I have made it very clear that we are out of money at the end of the month, and with COMDEX coming up a couple of weeks later, it would not be good if we had all our engineering staff disappear right before the show.

I continue to have little confidence and even lower esteem for our lead investor after all we've seen from him: his pettiness, his cluelessness as to what we actually do as a business, his skirt-chasing; he has funded us though, and for all these faults, we owe him our continued existence. It's been a miserable existence for me having to deal with him all this time, but if he brings us this two million dollar investment as promised, I think I can actually wipe the slate clean of my list of grievances and make a fresh start. "Hire him a hooker as a thank-you gift," Al suggested. "And make her French," added Jay.

I'll settle for closing on our big revenue deal and making him rich from his investment.

October 9th: Ninety-Day Budgets, Twenty Days' Funding

We might be slightly screwed here. I am thoroughly confused, that's for sure. Of course, I'd rather be confused than screwed, but I think when the clouds of confusion clear up, the forecast will be for a steady downpour of disaster.

The day began with our secondary investor requesting a ninety-day budget from me. I asked her what the parameters of the budget should be, since right now we have about three weeks of money in the bank, not three months; in the next month or so though, we're expecting the two million dollars in funding. Going from a few thousand to a few million dollars makes quite a difference to the budget numbers somewhere along that ninety-day timeline.

My confusion began when she asked what two million dollars I was referring to. It grew when she asked how we could only have three weeks of money left. She seemed perplexed when I explained the six-weeks of funding we had just received was for operations that began in mid-September after our layoffs; it's just that we didn't get to pay anyone for the second half of September until October 1st when we got the funds in the bank. Backdating the paychecks was something we had all agreed to at the time; apparently the investor's memory was not as true as the email exchanges between all of us Board members that confirmed this decision in mid-September.

My internal alarm bells were ringing: why would our secondary investor not be in the loop on the huge new funding injection we were about to receive? More to the point, why would she be expecting us to last three more months without additional funds? I thought perhaps she was planning to place three more months of bridge funding in place, hence the ninety-day budget request, but she said there was no more money to be placed, just an expectation that we would last on what we have.

So here I am, being asked to make three weeks' funding stretch three months: an impossibility, unless we have no employees and no offices for the next ninety days. I am pretty sure I would have remembered a meeting where I was told to shutdown the entire company—or a phone call, voicemail, email, or rock with a note attached flying through my window.

I decided to begin drawing up the budget, but to send an email out to both our investors asking (for the record) when we should expect whatever additional funding was to come in that would allow us to go three more months. No answer was forthcoming. This was worrying, so I called our lead investor to ask for an update on our two million dollars.

"What two million dollars?" he responded to my query. I must have paused for a good ten seconds, mouth agape, holding my breath and squeezing the phone as tightly as I would have liked to with my hands around his neck. I had no idea how to respond to his question. I mean what do you say? "The two million dollars you've been promising for months now." "The two million dollars I've been spending time writing budgets for and sending pages and pages of documentation out for." "The two million dollars I had a long conversation with your investor about the other day." Waiting for a response like: "Oh, *that* two million dollars. Sure, here you go. Cash or check?"

What I did get as a response was that the two million dollars was not looking likely. More like impossible.

The reason our beloved lead VC gave me is what officially screws us: his investor—the man with the checkbook who was going to fund him so he could fund us—that man...retired three days ago.

Maybe I should have figured this out myself, but you don't usually ask: "by the way, will you potentially be retiring between this conversation and writing us a check next week?" Maybe you do. Inexperience with the utterly bizarre seems to be my biggest handicap working with our VCs all this time.

Our lead investor may not be good at much of anything, but he really knows how to stage an excellent comedy of errors. We've covered everything from subtle irony to farce in one short act. The grand finale was the pie I just took in the face on that last phone call. Cue the curtain coming down.

October 20th: Teaching VCs to Use Email

I just had a premonition of my own death. One thing technology-focused venture capitalists seem incapable of is understanding how technologies work. In this case, it was our secondary investor, who apparently thought sending an email about me to our lead investor required her to put me on the 'To' list of the email as a recipient.

The email I received this morning suggested that I need to be replaced. The logic behind this decision from the secondary investor was made clear from the earlier emails included in the thread of correspondence. It all began with my ignored email to both investors enquiring about the two million dollar funding we were expecting. The investors had ignored me, but not the question, with the secondary investor asking the lead what I meant with my question. The lead investor—disingenuously—said he had no idea what I was talking about.

For our secondary investor, who has been too busy or too incompetent to pay any attention to our company, our funding situation or even what products we make, it is only natural to assume the company's CEO has gone a little insane to be asking about millions of dollars of phantom funding. I can't blame her for the suggestion to remove me on that basis, but can certainly point the finger at her lack of fiduciary responsibility as an investor and Board member in not knowing anything about the corporation she oversees.

It is certainly not for lack of trying or of data on the company. Beyond the monthly financial statements, and at this point, weekly budget documents and bank balances, the daily pleas for support or input on decisions could not have escaped her attention. They did escape responsiveness on her part, and were I an investor in her fund, just as with our lead investor, I would probably be looking very closely at whether this negligence was due to incompetence, indifference or malfeasance.

For my part, the investors had consistently steered us wrong, so while I took my duty to report all material facts on our status very seriously, I was more than happy to not have to follow their advice whenever possible. For the major decisions though, my hands were tied in required Board approval (which was rarely forthcoming). In particular, documents requiring signatures would never be endorsed or returned. In conjunction with our lawyers, we were forced to modify documentation style to only reflect my signature; documented notice and verbal approval from the investors became sufficient for many items, such as ratifying our Employee Stock Option Plan. Decisions we took in conference calls would be documented through an email from me summarizing the discussion, and a stated assumption that unless I heard differently, we were all implicitly confirming a Board mandate.

Documentation tricks of this sort have been an unanticipated encumbrance, delaying progress on many occasions, particularly when the window of opportunity is small to cut a deal, or enjoy some co-marketing benefit from a partner (all of our marketing must be pre-approved by the investors, so being mentioned in a partner press release requires a timely buy-in we can never rely on getting). They have created an excellent paper-trail though, and this would ordinarily be a great advantage in reviewing decisions and directives in logically arguing why we are in any given situation, and whose "fault" it might be. It would be a great advantage, if logic and facts had anything to do with our venture capitalists' thinking process.

Regardless of the volumes of documentation I have indicating I spent the last two months preparing for a large new funding round, including emails directly from our lead investor discussing it in graphic detail, he is able to simply say it never existed, and our other VC backs him.

It makes no difference in the end whether I can make the case that I am not delusional about the ghost of funding present; our relationship with our investors is at a point where we can't believe anything they say, and this makes it impossible to continue to operate as a viable business. My concern is that they might want to replace me, but without new funds in place, a new CEO still can't make us last three more months on three weeks' money. Nor do I believe any qualified executive is going to come in and replace me, given our situation, and the unreliable nature of our investors. Simply put, who in their right mind would want to replace me, with VCs like these?

October 23rd: VC Buddy #3: The BBQ CEO

Ask a silly question! We discovered who my replacement is to be. It's Mr. Calculator. CalcuMan. The guy we all rejected not too long ago as being completely useless: obviously not a critical factor in hiring him from our investors' point-of-view.

CalcuMan (Cal for short) showed up this morning, coming down from his home in Oregon. He is only staying for the day, though he'll be back here next week starting weekdays. Weekends, he intends to go back to Portland. He has no plans to move down here even temporarily, which is a surprise for someone trying to run a company, but is no surprise given our investors' history.

The best part was finding out exactly how our VCs had determined Cal was the man for the job. It turns out our lead investor's fund partner met Cal at a barbeque earlier this year. They chatted for a while, and Cal impressed him. That was it. No examination of his credentials, no review of his experience (or lack thereof) in running a company or knowing anything about our industry or about fund-raising.

The one thing our investors clearly responded to was Cal's unadulterated sliminess. We all recognized this when we interviewed him back in the summer, but he has clearly spent some time refining his abilities. I think everyone has experienced a co-worker who has no positive qualities or professional work ethic, but is a brilliant brown-noser, and is thus able to climb the corporate ladder by fawning on gullible managers and executives who like to have their egos stroked. As one colleague in a past company said to me about a useless former co-worker: "he is so far up his boss's ass, he found his colon cancer before the doctors did."

Despite Cal's obvious flaws, he appears to be here to stay, and as such I am willing to give him the opportunity to prove me wrong, get the company back on track and still make me rich in whatever position I now have. Speaking of which, Cal is replacing me, but no one has bothered to tell me what my job is now.

Cal's responsibilities are very clear, and I expect to judge him quickly and carefully on meeting them; he has three tasks: closing new revenue deals, closing new funding, and reducing our debt-load, as we have invoices and bills coming due that we cannot expect to pay off now that he is on-board and sucking the last of our money out for himself. He is being paid the equivalent of a quarter-million dollars a year, for twenty-hours a week of consulting. He is not an employee, even though he's acting-CEO, and is instead a consultant to our lead VC-firm, not to the corporation. This does not stop us from having to pay him and cover his health benefits out of our bank account, but apparently protects him from any potential legal actions that might be taken against the company, most likely by the very companies we can no longer pay because the allocated money is now going to him.

For a part-time employee, with no experience or qualifications for the job, not even living within five hundred miles of the office and who admitted to us that until this job, had been unemployed for a long time, unable to find any work and was struggling to pay the mortgage on his home in Oregon, Cal has done extremely well for himself. Just as with all the other venture buddies we have come across, his only skills seem to be schmoozing our investors and getting paid a ridiculous amount of (our) money for demonstrating his incompetence.

I'm willing to reserve judgement on Cal for now, but the one conclusion I have come to is that I need to spend more time at barbeques if I end up unemployed in a few weeks.

November 7th: Strike Three...You're Out!

I have had it with Cal. He has been here two weeks now, and every decision he has made has been destructive. Today though, he managed a new low with the single venture meeting he has gotten for us; it's his third strike though, and that means someone gets to call him out. That someone will be me.

Cal's first decision was to get rid of Al. Al is gone. One of the three co-founders of the company, and Cal decided to axe him, just like that. The investors have grumbled about Al for a long time, since he's the VP of Sales and so not landing more revenue deals falls on his shoulders. Al and I both agreed that we needed more sales, but the question has always been how we could do this. I was open to adding a new sales person or even replacing Al (which he was amenable to as he's become increasingly repulsed with our investors), but only on the basis that a newcomer could materially change things for the better. This was the same reasoning we used for my position too: I was happy to be replaced with someone who could bring in new funding, new revenues or reduce our debt-load in ways I would not be able to. None of these have happened of course; instead things have gotten much worse, much faster.

With Al gone, I passed on all the open deals we've been trying to close to Cal. Only he hasn't contacted a single one. I know this primarily because the customers have all been contacting me trying to figure out why we are suddenly ignoring them. In particular, our COMDEX partner wanted to confirm Al's presence at the show, to represent us as they sell their product (and ours bundled with it). With no Al, the onus is on Cal to take this slot. No response from Cal on that front yet.

Strike-one on Cal is that he is not getting us new revenue deals, and instead is making them less likely by ignoring customers.

Strike-two is on reducing our debt load. Cal gave a long speech to me the day he arrived on not ignoring our creditors who are seeking payments on their invoices (everyone from our landlords and the local phone company to a recruiting website that has an old outstanding bill from many moons ago when we were still looking to hire). The VCs had told us to ignore all invoices and bills, even though we suggested this was both unprofessional and likely to cause greater grief in the near future. On day one, when Cal seemed to agree with us, I was relieved and optimistic that he might actually do some good at least persuading the investors of the right course of action. Only he never followed up on a single debt we need to pay, and in the last couple of days, we started getting collection-notices and threats of legal action on our debts. What really did us in though was Cal not paying our rent for November. We have the money to do so, but Cal seems to have allocated all remaining money in the bank to himself, and if he gets paid, there's little left for anyone else. I should mention that we aren't being paid anymore, and the few remaining employees are done at the end of the week. We could have made it through November without Cal (perhaps even through December with a six-figure check expected from our continuing revenue deal); with Cal, and his need to have all his expenses and wages paid in advance, we are about to be made homeless. Our landlords have demanded we pay our rent, or leave the building immediately. Cal's response was to say it would take them a few months to legally oust us from the offices. Adding to our debt burden and legal woes is not what I expected from a competent replacement CEO hired to reduce or eliminate them.

Strike three came today. The only other responsibility for Cal is to bring in additional funding. Beyond not following up with any potential investor I gave him on my hit-list of funds I've been courting, he had suckered our current investors with tales of many VCs he was connected to and would bring to the table. This long list of investors has amounted to one VC from a fund I was unable to get any information on. Still, there are a lot of funds out there and as long as the guy had money I wasn't going to complain.

We were scheduled to meet Cal's contact this morning, in a hotel lobby near San Francisco airport. A little strange, but I figured the VC was not from the area, and was flying in to meet us. "No," Cal said, "he's from Sunnyvale." Sunnyvale is a Silicon Valley city not known as a venture capital hub but as a residential center; I would go as far as to suggest that no venture capitalist would ever willingly choose to be based in Sunnyvale, or be caught dead *in* Sunnyvale. So meeting in an airport hotel rather than in Sunnyvale sort of made sense but in a very troubling way about the quality and qualifications of the VC we were meeting.

Given this was our first venture meeting of the Cal era, I stopped by to ask Cal what kind of presentation he intended to give the VC, and whether he needed my assistance, since I was the one who did this in the past. I had already passed on the standard presentation and information package in software and hard-copy form that I used, for Cal to review and edit. It didn't look like Cal had bothered to even open the documents.

I suggested to Cal that if he wanted me to sit with him and go through the presentation, he could prep for the typical VC questions that would come up. I even offered to do the presentation at the meeting, if Cal felt uncomfortable representing the company at this point, since he knew so little about its intricacies. "There's no need," said Cal in response. "I have it all under control, you don't need to bring anything or even say anything. I'll do all the talking," he assured Jay and me as we sat with him. I shrugged and we left the room, assuming Cal had everything set to go. We were going to drive up together the following morning in our business-best and let Cal do his new job as CEO and fund-raiser.

Arriving at the airport hotel, it took us some time to track down Cal's friend, as the lobby area was bigger than anticipated. We finally tracked down the VC and found a quiet location with some couches into which we settled. All eyes were on Cal to make introductions and get on with the pitch.

Cal's opening statement was a tad unusual. He explained that he had been brought in to rescue our company due to the failures of management. Jay and I looked at each other in shock at this statement, and the VC raised an eyebrow. Why on earth would Cal be suggesting poor management to a VC he wanted to invest in the company, when the supposedly poor managers are sitting in front of him? Cal then told the investor that he wasn't all that familiar with the company yet, so he would have me give the investor pitch to the VC.

As the VC turned his attention to me, I looked quizzically at a confused Jay and then angrily at Cal. This was not what we had discussed. It made no sense. Cal was deliberately sabotaging us. He must have been. He set me up for a fall. Without presentation materials, I discussed the company as best I could, doing an adequate but uninspired job of promoting the company. I let myself be distracted by supposition of what Cal was up to and what he was likely to report to the VCs as my failure rather than his own.

The VC listened intently, and asked one or two standard questions; I knew from the moment Cal had suggested management problems though that he wasn't going to move forward.

When I completed my off-the-cuff presentation, the VC said he had gotten an understanding of our business, but recommended that if we seriously planned on raising money, we should put together a real presentation with slides and information for an investor to review. Cal nodded in agreement at this advice.

As we left and drove back down to the office (hoping we wouldn't be locked out of it by our landlords by now), I was fuming, but remained silent. Cal has a game plan, but so do I. This was strike-three, and I can now prove he has been unable to do accomplish anything in the three areas of responsibility he's been given.

This failure, coupled with the ridiculous cost of employing him should assure him a quick exit. Of course, this assumes the VCs are ready to hear the facts and make logical decisions. Not an assumption I really want to bet my company on.

November 11th: How to Piss Off an 800lb Gorilla

I have thus far been unable to sway our investors, but have swayed myself to end any spirit of cooperation between Cal and myself. The weird ambush he pulled with his VC friend made no sense to me, as any money we land with him aboard will of course be down to him, whether he has anything to do with it or not. So why he'd want us to fail is beyond me. Jay wonders if he has been sent in as some sort of Machiavellian terminator, making sure we are wiped out in some massive VC scheme involving kickbacks of the large sums of money Cal is currently allocating himself. I wouldn't put it past our lead investor to pull a scam like that. We always suspected the eighty thousand dollars our lead investor paid in legal expenses closing our first round due to the lawyer, Dick, was excessive. That we were not allowed to see the full invoices, and the VC netted out the money before funding us under the assumption they would pay Dick directly, made us all the more suspicious. At the time there was little we could do (I did demand the invoices, only to have it suggested this could delay the entire funding close were I to pursue it), but between this, and the many perk-laden trips expensed to us but with little value added or time dedicated to the company, our entire relationship was one VC kickback or misuse of funds after another, if we really wanted to scrutinize it.

So Cal continues to have the support of the VCs, regardless of my indications of his lack of any progress in any goal other than paying himself. This tends to suggest less about Cal and more about the investors. If someone was offering me free rein to clean out a company bank account while sitting around surfing the web and taking Bay Area friends out to lunch and dinner on an expense account, I might be tempted to do so myself. I'm not sure I could bring myself to do it, but with our investors, it might be a small act of retribution. Given Cal has no real history with our VCs that might require vengeance, I can only assume he's as amoral as his new masters.

In spite of all his political machinations, I had been willing to give Cal some time to get his act together, figuring it's hard to come into a new situation and hit the ground running, or determine whom he could trust within the organization. Perhaps he was simply sending me an unnecessary message that he is in control. That would explain the incompetence (he's not found his feet yet), and sabotage (a figurative horse's head at the foot of my bed). Thus I was willing to continue to work towards our common goals of reducing debts, land new funds and keep our deal pipeline moving forward, like a good soldier under a pompous general.

My opinion changed completely today though. It became abundantly clear that Cal has no idea what we are doing here, and more importantly, what he is doing here. After working for about twelve months on building a relationship with the world's largest company in our industry, Cal has decided in the space of a couple of weeks that he'd like us to now destroy that relationship over the next few days. He wants us to pull out of our COMDEX partnership a week before the start of the show. This is equivalent to bringing a ripe banana to the 800lb gorilla, and then sticking it up his nose. There's no coming back from a stunt like this.

Cal's fundamental reasoning appears to be that he doesn't want to work in a booth at COMDEX. Given he is the only one in the company getting paid; the only one who is allowed to represent the company to third parties now (the investors have put all decision-making in his greasy hands); and that we only have the funds to send one person to the show, it has to be Cal. He doesn't like the idea of having to do any actual work though, so he wants to pull out.

I attempted to explain the corporate suicide of pulling out at this point: our partner would have no way to replace us, and precious little time to remove us from their marketing materials and press releases. Beyond his lack of understanding of how serious a faux pas this would be, Cal believed it was advantageous to us, because our partner would be forced to promote us with their unchangeable marketing materials even as we no-showed.

I have to give Cal credit though; he is audacious in his rampant incompetence. He actually demanded that I contact our partner to let them know we were pulling out. I couldn't help but laugh at this suggestion, and as I walked out of his office, told him in no uncertain terms that he would need to do his own dirty work this time. It seems that this might have actually done the trick. Faced with damaging his personal credibility—"getting shit on his hands" as Al put it when I called to see how he was doing and he told me how much happier he was to be free of the daily misery I was filling him in on—Cal appears to have done an about-face and now believes the show is a "tremendous opportunity".

Suddenly though, I'm not sure what is worse: pulling out of the show or sending Cal to represent us. One thing is sure: it is a tremendous opportunity for Cal to finally prove me wrong and himself a winner, or add to his catalog of disastrous decisions and piss off the 800lb gorilla that currently holds our imminent corporate future in its hands.

November 22nd: Cleaning Out the Bank Account

Cal is quite a snake. Most likely a constrictor given his tenacious grip once he wraps his slithery body around your bank account.

Jay just called me, close to 10pm to say that Cal had just returned from Las Vegas. "Wow," I said, quite surprised. "He drove all the way back tonight after the show?" Cal had said he would save the company a lot of money by driving to Las Vegas rather than flying (particularly expensive the week of COMDEX, especially booking at the last minute), and that he had a sister who lived in Las Vegas and would stay with her during the show, thereby saving us even more money (hotel rooms the week of COMDEX could be over three hundred dollars per night). When I had heard these suggestions, I actually thought I had been overly harsh on the guy. As he prepared to drive off to Nevada, I wished him a lot of luck and told him we were on twenty-four hour standby should he need us for anything. After all, we were relying on him to come through for us at the show with deals, funding, some positive sign that could keep us in business beyond the next few weeks.

"He didn't drive, he flew," Jay informed me. "Not just that, but he left his rental car—the one he rented in Oregon before coming down to the Valley—in the short-term parking at the San Jose airport." I was trying to fathom why he would do this rather than return the car and get another at the airport when he got back a week later. I was trying hard not to think about the cost of buying a same-day ticket to Las Vegas.

"It gets better," Jay continued. "He didn't stay with his sister, he booked a hotel room and he even rented another car while in Las Vegas." I didn't know how to respond. It was like Cal was seeing if he could fit every possible stupid decision a person could make into this one trip.

"So did Cal call you to let you know he was back in town?" I asked. Jay laughed ruefully: "He did more than that. He called me repeatedly, demanding that I meet him at the bank, and take out cash to pay off his expenses immediately. He seemed concerned that there wouldn't be enough in there to cover his travel expenses if he waited."

"So why not just go with you tomorrow?" I asked, already fearing I knew why. "Because he's flying back to Oregon tonight, which, by the way, he also included on his travel expenses." I could sense Jay shaking his head as I heard him sigh deeply into the phone. How the hell did we end up with this loser? Oh yeah, because of the other losers he reports to.

There's not much we can do at this point. Jay said Cal was particularly angry because he was limited to a one thousand dollar withdrawal from the ATM for the day. He demanded Jay write him a check for an additional three thousand dollars to cover the rest of his trip expenses. He anticipated filing additional costs associated with his meals and entertainment expenses when he got back to Oregon.

The four thousand dollars Cal managed to rack up alone had been enough to send five employees to last year's COMDEX show. This time around though, four thousand dollars may well have cleaned out our bank account completely. Which I'm guessing was Cal's intention all along.

November 25th: Enough

Today I officially resigned my position as President and Chairman of the Board of Directors of my corporation. I have had enough. My resignation was partly in disgust, partly because I've seen enough financial mismanagement and malfeasance to believe there's a real liability risk in continuing to be a corporate officer, particularly as we have a growing list of creditors sending demand notices and threatening to sue us.

Of particular concern are the subtle manipulations of history being attempted by the investors, clearly attempting to suggest mismanagement by the company founders. I am almost hoping they try to pursue this. One thing I have been adamant about is documenting everything and maintaining a scrupulous paper trail. I have the goods on everyone, and while I have no compunction to use any of it, it'll be my bulletproof vest should the firing begin.

The last straw for me was the conversation I had tonight with our lead investor's partner. In my limited experiences with him, he had always seemed quite reasonable. On the other hand, he was the barbeque co-conspirator with Cal, recommending his hiring as my replacement. With our Board members refusing to discuss Cal, or pretty much anything with me at this point, I finally had a heart-to-heart with the lead's partner, letting him know my reasons for considering Cal to be a liability to the company, and suggesting that we needed at least a course correction if not an exorcism. Having acknowledged that Cal had not met any of his responsibilities, and accepting he had pretty much cleaned out our bank account under false pretenses (Cal had maintained his altruistic story of driving to Vegas and sleeping on his sister's couch to the investors), the VC partner endorsed his continued presence.

Logic, reason, evidence were not going to affect our situation, and the absence of these mean the absence of me too. It makes little sense to be party to the destruction of what we worked so hard to build, particularly when the sabotage is an inside job.

The only way the death spiral will stop (perhaps pause is more accurate) turns out to be the most ironic thing: with our bank account cleared out, Cal does not plan on sticking around beyond the end of the month. The investors of course are unaware of this fact, and they will soon be forced back into dealing with us directly, or forking out for Cal's services in what is certainly a lost cause without us.

Given past history, I believe they'll choose the latter, and will pay dearly for their decision. It'll just take them a while to realize they'll be doing so in more ways than just the money.

January 1st: Happy New Year!

The New Year brings the same old challenges. Despite warning our investors repeatedly that there are many end-of-year filings required of the corporation, not to mention many open action items that needed to be closed prior to January 1st to avoid incurring fees for the forthcoming year, it took until today for them to act.

Not that they acted of course. They brought back an old friend to do that. Cal has returned, no doubt with an even more inflated compensation package on which we could have actually operated the company for a few more months.

Cal is in no mood to start the New Year by working for a living though, and has instead recruited an impoverished Jay to do his dirty work for him. I don't blame Jay for acquiescing, but he is being paid about ten percent of Cal's fee for doing one hundred percent of Cal's work. I recommended Jay approach the VCs directly and cut out the middleman; instead he is stuck self-admittedly carrying all the workload but just playing pack-mule to Cal. (Cal though, continues to play the ass.)

The biggest surprise to me is that the investors continue to back a malicious incompetent, simply to avoid having to speak to my fellow co-founders or me. I suppose you're willing to pay a great deal of money to avoid getting your hands dirty or face the truth. Venture capital is all about wishful thinking in essence: taking an idea on the back of a napkin and turning it into a billion-dollar company. You just hope there's more than wishful thinking behind the VCs you partner with; any thinking would be a good start.

As I begin the New Year, I do have one accomplishment I can look back at with pride. Four million dollars over three years never bought my soul, and though my company may be penniless, we were never financially or morally bankrupt. I doubt our venture capitalists can say the same.

February 2nd: Out

I am out. Officially, as of this day, I no longer have any connection to the company I conceived, birthed and bottle-fed for three years. The final ignominy was the VCs' demand that as founders, we return our stock holdings, or be forced to pay upwards of fifty thousand dollars to purchase the stock we had always held in our own company. One of those nasty little clauses that I had tried unsuccessfully to negotiate out was our undoing. At this point, I am more relieved to be free of any and all ties that I was almost glad to sign over my stock. I did manage to document the fact I was essentially being forced to do so under duress, which does actually offer me legal protections later on should I wish to reclaim my holdings in the future. Why I would ever want to do so is beyond me. The intellectual property is so opaque to our investors and to their bagman Cal, that it is worthless.

In fact the IP is valuable and will be more so in times ahead as the market catches up to the forward-looking solutions we developed for a future industry that is only now establishing itself. However, I have no reason to point that out to the sole owners now, and in fact am delighted that they know nothing about what they might be sitting on, despite numerous efforts over time to explain and document our solution for exactly this purpose.

So this is it. The end. Quite an anticlimactic moment, to be honest. I somehow expected fireworks; or an elaborate funeral; instead it was simply signing some final paperwork and walking away. The investors themselves have not been in direct contact with me for months. I occasionally hear from Jay who is continuing to do their bidding for the scraps they toss at him, but which he needs to feed and house his family. It's easier to be moralistic when you don't have kids.

The investor's on-going incompetence and negligence has led to many extraneous fees and fines racking up for a corporation that has been completely wound-down, except to file the final documents to strike it off the books. It is somehow comforting to know that the same things that struck us as stupid the first day I met our venture capitalists in Chicago are still alive and well three plus years later. We've gone from three poor guys in a room with an idea to a company of forty employees and millions of dollars in the bank, and reduced now to no guys in no room. And through it all, our venture capitalists stood as an immoveable monument to financial, moral, ethical and personal corruption.

I should have been more worried that first day in Chicago…but it really was hard to argue with two million dollars. And now, years later, I may not be rich, but I am far richer for the experience: the employees and colleagues I was lucky enough to work with, the partners and customers I sold our vision to along the way, and the business I was able to build from nothing and sustain at least for a little while.

I wouldn't change a thing from these last few years of ups and downs…except perhaps all the people, places and events related to that wild investor ride that made up our Adventure Capital.

The End.

EPILOGUE: *Lessons Learned*

My entrepreneurial experience was unfortunate, but not atypical. In fact, it's said that the average entrepreneur has seven failures before they run a successful company. This is a testament to how difficult achieving success can be, and how dedicated your 'average' entrepreneur is to making it.

Even a failed company teaches many lessons; reviewing the mistakes made so as not to repeat them is how each corporate experience brings you ever closer to success.

Author and publisher Michael Korda has said:

> *"Never walk away from failure. On the contrary, study it carefully—and imaginatively—for its hidden assets".*

In that spirit, I highlight here the lessons I learned from my failure. I hope that many an entrepreneur can borrow my failed company as one of the seven they'll have in their lifetime, and save themselves some time and heartache.

Lesson 1: Don't Ignore the Warning Signs
Lesson 2: Listen to Experts
Lesson 3: Run Your Company
Lesson 4: Chase Success, Not Money
Lesson 5: The Buddy System
Lesson 6: Trails of Paper
Lesson 7: Look Back Fondly

Lesson 1: Don't Ignore the Warning Signs

I had alarm bells ringing the first day I met the man who was to become our lead venture investor. The need for money and the belief that the situation was manageable overrode the alarm. The next three years of my life—business and otherwise—was consumed with operating my company while dodging obstacles in the maze of distraction our VCs placed us in.

Whether you seek an equity investment or a loan, terms and lenders that look great when you are in desperate need may bring you down more painfully and catastrophically than walking away in the first place would. That VCs thrive on entrepreneurial desperation—waiting until your company is at its most impoverished—to give themselves the strongest negotiating position only makes it that more important you have a positive working relationship early on. If you are out raising additional capital from new investors applying the same rule of waiting until you are out of money, the last thing you want is to be battling your current VCs at the same time.

I can categorically say that our choice of lead investor shaped our entire corporate history, and in profoundly negative ways. There truly are such things as bad money and dumb money; you *must* sail your corporate ship clear of them, in spite of their siren call to fund you, lest your hopes be dashed on a rocky venture relationship you can't escape from later.

There's an old phrase: "marry in haste, regret in leisure". Hold that truth close to you as you raise any kind of funding, and pay heed to those gut feelings, inner alarm bells and your nose telling you when something smells bad.

Lesson 2: Listen to Experts

A corollary to Lesson 1: if you have experts involved in your funding process, as we did with our excellent, experienced lawyers, listen to what they are telling you. We choose experts for a reason, but too often hope they simply reinforce what we already believe, or endorse the actions we are already taking, rather than challenge us through experiential wisdom.

In my case, our law firm had grave reservations about our venture capital partners, and on more than one occasion asked: "are you sure you want to do business with these people?" Blinded by our need for money and assuming all venture capitalists would be driving hard bargains and being adversarial in a funding process, we ignored these warnings. That our lawyers cautioned us that our investors were not operating like any other VC and in fact were highly atypical did not matter to us at the time. We made a fundamental mistake, which was to seek out and secure tremendous expertise at significant cost; and then not heed their expert counsel when offered, and when we really needed to. It is your responsibility alone to take an executive decision as a business-owner, but it is also your responsibility to make it an informed decision by seeking input from the trusted advisors around you.

Paying attention early on: "we're telling you how bad this is" can mean avoiding hearing: "we told you so," when it is too late.

Lesson 3: Run Your Company

This is an easy lesson in theory, but a difficult one in practice, particularly for first time entrepreneurs in a venture environment. It is *your* company, and you need to be the one running it. Not just on a day-to-day operational level, but in strategic direction, long range positioning and focus.

As a first time CEO, I relied heavily on our venture capitalists to offer me advice. Expert advice I believed they had over me from their experience as investors in multiple startups. This is a fundamental problem with Lesson Two above: listening to experts only works when they truly are experts. Beyond being sure you are getting good advice to act on, you must determine whether you are getting skewed advice too. Not all venture capitalists are as incompetent as mine were, but all venture capitalists have their own focus on maximizing a return on their investment, and minimizing the time to reach an exit where they can realize that return. For the most part, the milestones that grow your business and achieve that exit are common. However, there are times where chasing a short-term goal can be key for a VC and a distraction to your core business as an entrepreneur.

Recognizing when advice is good for you, good for your investors, or good for both of you is difficult but vital. Once determined, you need to move the corporation in ways that benefit you or everyone, but not just your investors. This can eventually lead to conflict; but if you are firm in the belief that you are doing what is best for the company—*your* company—then you have a defensible position. Requiring your investors to prove they are doing the same can lead to a healthy debate that may offer a compromise solution or even a better path forward.

In the end, you are the best person at running your company, and abdicating that responsibility would be a terrible mistake. Lead from the front, don't wait for crises to drive decisions, and don't wait for your Board or your investors to give direction. Determine when a decision needs to be made, request input and validate your choice based on known facts on the ground at the time. Listening to your gut (Lesson One), and weighing expert advice from everyone including your investors (Lesson Two) are how you do this successfully. You won't always be correct, but your decision-making process in running your company always will be.

Lesson 4: Chase Success, Not Money

Startup companies in the Dotcom era were all about only one thing: money. Of course, all companies are about money in the end, that is why they are in business after all. Companies are not *all* about money though: they are about products, services, customers, the things that lead to revenues and money.

As a venture-backed startup, our milestones were always cast in terms of the next investment imperative. What will it take to raise our next round of funding? What will increase our valuation enough for a new investor to fund us? Of course we looked to land deals and bring in revenue, but only to help raise more money. This is not the way to build a business. Instead of looking upon venture capital as a source of money to operate the company to achieve growth milestones, we were looking to grow the company as a way to achieve new funding milestones. Completely backwards. It's a very simple lesson, but one that makes a fundamental difference, and affects your entire strategy as a business.

Part of our falling into this trap was the environment we were in, part of it was in our reliance on letting our venture capitalists guide our thinking on what our goals should be, but mostly it was a rookie mistake as first time entrepreneurs caught up in a money-chase rather than executing a business-plan that we had established on paper but were constantly distracted from. We could see venture-capital candy-houses all around us and seemingly get to them if we just strayed off the path a little bit into the forest. Only each one was inhabited by a witch, trios of bears or a granny-devouring wolf, and finding our way back to the path was a little bit harder every time we left it, as we became ever more desperate and darkness fell all around us.

A good entrepreneur has more than riches in mind when they start their business. They have dreams of bringing new products or services to customers who wouldn't be able to do without them if they only knew they existed, and a plan to make those dreams a reality. Remember those dreams, remember those plans whenever you are tempted to stray from the path, and ask yourself if the shortcut through the woods you're about to take will truly lead you where you want to go.

Lesson 5: The Buddy System

Beyond cash in the bank, good venture capitalists are judged by their ability to open doors and bring in experts you would otherwise have no way of reaching. Bad venture capitalists have a similar ability, which is to funnel high-priced idiots and shysters to your company. Accepting dumb money from a bad VC is one thing, but don't let them foist bad people on you.

We had more than our share of incompetent or malfeasant venture capitalist buddies, just as we saw many suspect equity investors seeking only to put money into businesses operated by buddies inside their known network. Most importantly, our venture capitalists had a detrimental effect on the business directly, but more fundamentally, the personnel they placed into positions of power or influence affected our chances of success more tangibly and effectively.

Not all VC buddies are bad necessarily, but all buddies of bad VCs should be treated with suspicion. Anyone brought in as a high-priced consultant needs to prove their worth. If you brought in your buddies on expensive contracts, your investors would be asking serious questions. Hold your VCs to the same standard, and don't be afraid to challenge paying for incompetence. I didn't, and the results were unplanned (our business-plan writer), désastreux (le buddy), and incalculable (the BBQ buddy and calculator salesman CEO) respectively.

Lesson 6: Trails of Paper

Document everything. That's pretty much all there is to this lesson. Having a paper-trail is essential if you start spinning down a death-spiral with venture capitalists who need to pin the blame on someone if they have a failed investment on their hands.

Documenting decisions, processes and conversations has little operational value if your investors don't deal in logic as ours didn't, but is a logical and sensible decision to make in protecting yourself in the worst-case. Preparing for the worst while hoping for the best is the eternal motto of the entrepreneur. Protecting yourself, your employees and your corporation from being usurped (by anyone including yourself, your employees and the corporation and its investors) is vital. As E.L. Kersten once said:

"The secret of success is knowing whom to blame for your failure."

Documentation and a paper-trail counter this eloquently sage quotation with the more colloquial abbreviation: "CYA": Cover Your Ass.

Lesson 7: Look Back Fondly

"Successful men usually snatch success from seeming failure. If they know there is such a word as defeat, they will not admit it. They may be whipped, but they are not aware of it. That is why they succeed."

A.P. Gouthey's words from over five hundred years ago still stand today.

The hardest thing for an entrepreneur to do is to admit defeat. In my case, my company was on its last legs longer than it was standing fit and tall in its four years of existence. You will scrape and claw your way to survive as long as you can, and this is commendable and an essential trait of the good businessperson. Sometimes though, you need to know when you're licked, and add one to the list of failures you need to get through to become that eighth-time's-a-charm success.

Regardless of success or failure, however, enjoy the experience. Even when things are miserable, even on the worst days, you are running your own company, chasing your own dreams, master of your own future. For all my misery—documented in great detail in this book—I never regret my decision to have founded and operated my own startup. The people I worked with—the psychos, prima donnas, over-medicated and under-medicated, committed and ought-to-be-committed, somber, sober and silly—the whole motley crew were a joy to be around. I don't know what they think of their CEO today, but I love every one of them. We did more than share an office—we shared a dream, even if for some, it was just a job to pick up a paycheck. I choose to believe they bought into the dream just a little bit, just a little while. I hope so at least, because life would be pretty miserable otherwise. I often said my goal was to make my employees millionaires (making myself a multi-millionaire in the process of course). None of us are millionaires yet…but there's always next time.

"There is no failure except in no longer trying."
[Elbert Hubbard]

0-595-34461-5

www.ingramcontent.com/pod-product-compliance
Lightning Source LLC
Chambersburg PA
CBHW030752180526
45163CB00003B/995